T0243232

Advance Praise for *The Path of an Eagle*

"Jay's willingness to vulnerably share his truth will change you forever. When you witness someone live their truth, it gives you permission to do the same. I highly recommend this book!"

Gabby Bernstein, *#1 New York Times* Bestselling Author of *The Universe Has Your Back*

"Jay's stories will grip you, move you, and inspire you. *The Path of an Eagle* is one for the story lovers and those searching for wisdom, truth, and real connection in their lives."

Mel Robbins, *New York Times* Bestselling Author of *The High 5 Habit* and *The 5 Second Rule,* World Renowned Motivational Speaker

"Jay Fantom is an incredibly inspiring Australian. Anyone who wants to know how to recover from setbacks or trauma will be inspired by this beautiful book."

Johann Hari, *New York Times* Bestselling Author of *Chasing The Scream* and *Lost Connections*

"This book is spreading such a powerful message out to the world. It's full of useful strategies and resources to help you overcome whatever challenge you may face in your life. Definitely worth a read!"

Nick Vujicic, *New York Times* Bestselling Author, World Renowned Speaker, Coach, and Entrepreneur

"This is a book that the world needs. We need more young voices who can show us all what it takes to overcome life's greatest challenges and lead forward. By being honest, open, courageous, and vulnerable with us, Jay's stories will not only inspire, but also give you everything you need to live the best life possible. I highly recommend this book!"

Atticus Poetry, *New York Times* Bestselling
Author and Award-Winning Poet

"A must read! *The Path of an Eagle is* a journey of self-discovery and one brave young man's fight to rise above tragedy and become a light for those struggling in the darkness. Kudos to Jay for having the courage to share deeply personal, vulnerable experiences which served to help the reader to understand the struggles of a young male—which oddly, were not so different from the struggles I and so many other young women have endured."

Tana Amen, B.S.N, R.N. *New York Times* Bestselling
Author of *The Omni Diet, The Relentless Courage
of a Scared Child,* and VP, Amen Clinics

"Real and authentic are the two words that will burst into your mind as you read *The Path of an Eagle.* The stories Jarred shares about his own experiences will not only challenge you, but also inspire you to become better in your own life. This is a must-read for anyone wanting to grow and reach their full potential."

Dr. Nicole LePera, *New York Times*
Bestselling Author of *How to Do the Work*

"*The Path of an Eagle* is filled with many heartfelt and inspiring stories from Jay's life. This book will take you down the right paths toward healing your mind and heart from the unthinkable. It's a must-read!"

Dr. Caroline Leaf, Communication Pathologist and Neuroscientist, *New York Times* Bestselling Author

"In *The Path of an Eagle*, Jay shares a real and vulnerable look at his story—and in our world full of highlight reels, it's much needed. He offers the inspiration, encouragement, and truth that anyone who feels knocked down needs to hear. Whether or not you're experiencing that kind of season, this book can help set you up for mental, emotional, and spiritual success."

Dr. Will Cole, Leading Functional Medicine Expert, *New York Times* Bestselling Author of *Intuitive Fasting*

"If you have ever struggled in your life to get back up after you've been knocked down by life's challenges, then this book is for you! It will give you everything you need to overcome whatever hardship comes your way. This is a must-read!"

Amy Purdy, *New York Times* Bestselling Author, Motivational Speaker, and Athlete

"Jay packs so many inspiring well-told stories in *The Path of an Eagle*. These authentic stories are sure to help you rise above challenges and difficult times in your life. I highly recommend reading this book and gifting it to your friends and family."

Nikki Sharp, Bestselling Author of *The 5-Day Detox*

"*The Path of an Eagle* is a powerful book that provides hope and strategies in the form of well-told stories that enable anyone to overcome the most difficult of obstacles. If you want to live a healthy life—you have chosen the right book to help on your journey."

Dr. Josh Axe, Bestselling Author of
Ancient Remedies and *Eat Dirt*

"What a rollercoaster ride Jay takes you on in *The Path of an Eagle*. Just when you think the story ends, there's more! This is more than a self-help book. It's a roadmap to help you overcome and lead forward in your life. It's a must-read!"

Chris Norton, Bestselling Author of *The 7 Longest Years*

"Jay Fantom's *The Path of the Eagle* is a riveting narrative. Teeming with loving, actionable steps, Jay leads the reader out from any point of personal pain and despair into the truth of each person's God-given blessings, purpose, inner strength, self-worth, and love. If you are ready to experience transformation change, this book's gripping raw stories and enlightened wisdom will guide you there. It is a fast read but an indelible gift."

Nancy J Ganz, Bestselling Author and
Founder of Feel Good Fables

"Insightful, inspiring, and powerful. *The Path of an Eagle* shows you exactly what it takes to get back up after being knocked down."

Horst Schulze, Co-Founder of The Ritz Carlton
Hotel and Bestselling Author of *Excellence Wins*

"Jay has a heart for service that is very apparent in this book, teaching others to rise above the trauma or pain they have experienced, and to help others who might have experienced something similar."

Serena Poon, Celebrity Chef, Certified
Nutritionist, and Reiki Master

"Riveting, inspiring, insightful! *The Path of an Eagle* is the courageous story of a young man's journey of finding triumph over trauma. This MUST-READ book is for anyone looking for inspiration to transform their life after being knocked down by life's challenges."

Susan Zinn, Licensed Psychotherapist,
Certified Trauma Specialist, Author, and
Founder of Westside Counselling Centre

"I absolutely love how this book shows the true power of turning our pain into gain for others through our personal stories! And the way Jay ties in the leadership and love of Jesus, EPIC!!!"

David Nurse, NBA Life Optimization Coach,
Motivational Keynote Speaker, and Bestselling Author

"Our brains need stories of how others have flourished within their constraints so we might know our own hard stories can be ones of flourishing too. Jay poignantly offers himself and the valuable lessons he's learned to us as a reminder that often life's most difficult struggles can also be our most powerful assignments."

Katherine and Jay Wolf, Survivors, Advocates,
Bestselling Authors of *Suffer Strong* and *Hope Heals*

"With an authentic and heartfelt voice, Jay Fantom gives readers a transformational plan to soar to new heights. There's no better time than now to benefit from this book."

Derrick Kinney, Author of *Good Money Revolution*
and Host of the *Good Money* podcast

"Jay's book is a story of transforming pain to purpose. It is one of the most honest books I have read about people going through real life challenges and being truly resilient! In today's times, stories of people's resiliency are stories everyone can learn and benefit from!"

MaryRuth Ghiyam, Bestselling Author of *Liquids Till Lunch* and Founder of MaryRuth Organics

"This is one of the most honest books I've ever read. Jay's willingness to speak his truth, and his determination to overcome adversity, are truly inspirational. If you're in need of hope, growth, and inspiration, this is the book for you."

Dr. Sarah Woodhouse, Bestselling Author of *You're Not Broken*, Research Psychologist, and Trauma Expert

"Eagles don't flock, and neither should you. Jay's book will inspire you at the depth of your being to be an eagle that manifests your full destiny and accomplishing great and wonderful things."

Mark Victor Hansen, World's Bestselling Author of the *Chicken Soup* and *ASK!* book series

THE PATH OF
AN EAGLE

HOW TO
OVERCOME
AND LEAD
AFTER BEING
KNOCKED DOWN

JAY FANTOM

A POST HILL PRESS BOOK
ISBN: 978-1-63758-492-7
ISBN (eBook): 978-1-63758-493-4

The Path of an Eagle:
How to Overcome and Lead After Being Knocked Down
© 2022 by Jay Fantom
All Rights Reserved

The moral rights of the author of this work have been asserted.

All rights reserved. No part of this book may be reproduced or transmitted in any form or by any means, electronic or mechanical, including photocopying, recording, or by any information storage and retrieval system, without prior permission in writing from the publisher. The Australian Copyright Act 1968 (the Act) allows a maximum of one chapter or 10 percent of this book, whichever is the greater, to be photocopied by any educational institution for its educational purposes provided that the educational institution for its educational purposes provided that the educational institution (or body that administers it has given a remuneration notice to the Copyright Agency (Australia) under the Act.

This is a work of nonfiction. All people, locations, events, and situations are portrayed to the best of the author's memory. Although every effort has been made to ensure that the personal and professional advice present within this book is useful and appropriate, the author and publisher do not assume and hereby disclaim any liability to any person, business, or organization choosing to employ the guidance offered in this book.

No part of this book may be reproduced, stored in a retrieval system, or transmitted by any means without the written permission of the author and publisher.

Scripture quotations taken from The Holy Bible, New International Version®
NIV® Copyright © 1973 1978 1984 2011 by Biblica, Inc. TM
 Used by permission. All rights reserved worldwide.

Post Hill Press
New York • Nashville
posthillpress.com

Published in the United States of America
1 2 3 4 5 6 7 8 9 10

This one's for you—Grandy, Grandma, Joy, and Missy. Thank you for continuing to watch over me. Until I see you all again someday soon.

CONTENTS

FOREWORD

by Tana Amen
(*New York Times* bestselling author)

The Path of an Eagle is more than a self-help book. This is a story of transforming pain to purpose. Jay's life story will astound you, inspire you, and help you realize you are not alone in your struggles.

As someone who has overcome significant childhood and adult trauma, I was enthralled by Jay's story and life lessons. Despite our obvious differences, I was again reminded that people have more in common than we dare to imagine. Regardless of your gender, race, or circumstances in which you were raised, we all suffer from the human condition.

As a woman who is old enough to be Jay's mother, I was amazed how much I could relate to nearly every part of his story. His courage to share deeply personal, vulnerable experiences is commendable and helped me understand the struggles of a young male—which oddly, were not so different from the struggles I endured as a young female.

At Amen Clinics, we believe that illness and healing occur in four circles:

- Biology: the physical functioning of your brain and body
- Psychology: how you manage your mind

- Social: your connections to other people (people are contagious)
- Spiritual: your purpose for being on the planet

The circles are much like tires on a car. If one tire goes flat, the car won't drive very far. If more than one tire goes flat, the car will likely crash. Jay's roller-coaster life story is the perfect example of why healing needs to occur in all four circles to sustain healing.

Like Jay, I have experienced the pain of having a serious imbalance in each of these circles. Only when care is given to balance each area of life will we finally recognize our true purpose and meet our potential.

The Path of an Eagle is a journey of self-discovery and one brave young man's fight to rise above tragedy and become a light for those struggling in the darkness. Through his experiences and story, Jay shares his steps for success.

Tana Amen, B.S.N, R.N.
NYT Bestselling Author of *The Omni Diet*
and *The Relentless Courage of a Scared
Child*, VP at Amen Clinics

WORDS OF THANKS AND ACKNOWLEDGMENTS

If I were to thank everyone who has inspired this book, it would take another book just to thank all of them. I am extremely grateful for each person who has been there for me through the ups and the downs in my life.

I firstly and most importantly want to thank God for enriching my story with countless blessings, never-ending joy, trials, and love. Thank you for placing me on the path of an eagle and for giving me the strength to hope in you and soar high in my life.

To my wonderful, hardworking parents, John and Fiona. It is difficult to put into words just how thankful I am to you both for the way you raised me. I love you to heaven and back again.

My brothers, Nathan and Jonathan, I'm grateful for your support over the years; I may not say it enough, but I love you both.

To Uncle Paul, the man who inspired me to get into film in the first place. Thank you for all your support, guidance, and love over this crazy journey.

To Grandy and Grandma, I truly wish that you both could be here to experience my growth and be part of my life. You were both taken too soon. I will forever honor and carry on all the advice you gave to me and spread it far and wide to make you proud. I can't wait to see you both again. Keep on soaring up in heaven for me. And please give Joy and Missy a hug for me too.

I also want to say thank you to my editor Michele Perry from Wordplay Editing Services for seeing my vision and taking it to newfound heights. I am grateful for all the support and guidance you provided along this fun process, answering all my questions and calming my nerves. Thank you to Michael Francis McDermott, who connected me with Michele. You are golden, my friend.

Tana Amen, thank you so much for writing the foreword of this book. For you continued support, love, and friendship—it means more to me than this side of eternity can show. Thank you for saying yes.

To Gabby Bernstein. Thank you for giving me that extra push that I needed to jump-start my creativity. You are awesome.

To those people who agreed to endorse my book—I honor your words, sincerity, time, and generosity, and I will forever be in your debt.

To my publisher, Post Hill Press, thank you for getting this book out into the world and for giving me a chance. You turned a dream of mine into a reality. Thank you, Debra Englander, for seeing my book as something special and for believing in me. Thank you to the incredible team who worked tirelessly behind the scenes. Heather King, thank you for putting up with my constant emails and asks, you are a Godsend. To Devon Brown for all your work with publicity, thank you for giving it your all!

Emily Baird, you beautiful human being you! We did it! Thank you from every ounce of my being for your persistent efforts and your infectious never give up attitude. Thank you for believing in me and *The Story Box*. We are the dream team!

For every single person that has been a part of *The Story Box* and believed in me, I just want to say I am deeply humbled by your generosity, friendship, support, and kindness. Without your sacrifice, I wouldn't be where I am today.

KEEP ON SOARING

INTRODUCTION

> "Those who *hope* in the Lord will renew
> their strength. They will *soar* on the wings
> like Eagles; they will run and not grow
> weary; they will *walk* and not be faint."
> Isaiah 40:31

It's Time for You to Soar

Dear reader, whatever you are going through in your life—whether it be good or bad—I know that this book will help you.

When I originally sat down at my desk with my old iPad Pro in 2019, I wrote from a place of pain. Because that's what I was in—a lot of pain and feeling like I was suffering. My life wasn't going anywhere. I felt stuck and depressed, and as a result that made me feel utterly miserable every day. I had no direction in my life.

I never thought that my stories would eventually end up in your hands today. Because, to be completely honest with you all, I gave up writing altogether following the completion of my first draft. I was so ashamed of it, and I allowed these horrible, negative thoughts to take control of my life. This way of thinking only plunged me further into that sinking pit of despair and misery, where I have no doubt some of you are right now.

I naively thought that by writing everything I was feeling and going through, then maybe it would become a *New York Times* bestselling book. (I know, it makes me laugh too!) But as I discovered, not everything you write can become a book—let alone a bestselling one.

I selfishly didn't have you (my reader) in mind at all when I first started writing. It was all about me and what I was feeling. It was only when I decided to erase my blinding ego out of the equation that I was able to see the path ahead with more clarity.

And so I started again, but this time with a renewed perspective, vision, and heart aimed at wanting to share some of my stories to help you overcome and lead yourself through the difficulties, the challenges, the pain, the suffering, the broken relationships, the addictions, the hate, the sinking feelings, the negative emotions, the depression, the anxiety, the stress, the traumas, all the while offering you a unique, healing path forward.

There will be moments as you read on that will send chills down your spine. Moments when you think to yourself, *how on earth is Jay still here?* There are stories that will not only be helpful but keep you interested and asking yourself *what else can I learn next?* And just when you think a story is over…it's not.

I often equate life to that of a roller-coaster ride. The slow grinding steep slopes, the fast downward spirals, or even those sharp turns and jagged edges. Sometimes you want to vomit, while other times you get excited.

So, strap yourself in because it's going to be one heck of a great ride!

This isn't a religious book, although my faith in God does form a large part of my life and identity. I'm not ashamed about it at all, and I'm proud to proclaim his name. I wouldn't be here if it weren't for him. All that I am today and the man I have become is because of God. I owe him everything and he owes me nothing, yet he always gives.

He has given me a great story to share with you all. He has also given me insight, profound knowledge, understanding, and wisdom well beyond my years, which I am eternally grateful for and wouldn't change for all the money in the world.

I know there are people out there (and you may even be one of them) who have gone through far worse than what I have, and I'm certainly not trying to take away from your story at all. In fact, I want to do the complete opposite! I want to amplify your voice and story. I'd like to encourage you to share it. You, my dear reader, have a unique story. And in case no one has ever told you this before, it's incredibly valuable!

We may never know the impact our stories can have on someone else, but that should only encourage us to be bold enough to share them. Do you agree?

I firmly believe that when we choose to lead forward with courage, empathy, and kindness, and when we share our most vulnerable stories with others, it can help others, as well as ourselves, heal. That's the true power of stories, and I've seen them in action on my podcast, *The Story Box*.

I consider it selfish not sharing my story with people.

So, what I would like you to ask yourself is: *who am I to hold onto something so precious that could impact someone else in a positive way?* You might not be ready to share and that is fine. But please don't stop yourself from thinking about it.

The eagle is a symbol and picture of hope and leadership. Please keep that in mind as you take this journey with me. And remember that eagles weren't created for the ground. They were designed for a special purpose like you were: to soar high above the clouds, reaching for the heavens and newfound heights. When faced with difficult circumstances, the eagle remains ever present and focused. It's determined to spread its mighty wings and take flight, navigating through the harshest storms. That when beaten down, it doesn't stay down. The eagle rises back up and chooses to soar higher than it did before.

Eagles love to embrace challenges because they know that these challenges make them more effective leaders. In fact, eagles get excited about what's next.

I only wish that I had had these stories and the wisdom that they carry available to me at a younger age. Maybe I might have been able to overcome a lot of the suffering I endured earlier. But this side of eternity, I'll never know.

However, I do pray that you—my new friend—consider with an open heart and mind what my stories, and the stories, lessons, and wisdom of others mentioned in this book, have to offer you. These others, like me, have decided to walk down a path that leads to fulfilment, unspeakable joy, learning, and growth.

What is this path called, you may ask.

Well, I like to call it…

The path of an eagle.

Will you join me in walking down this path?

CHAPTER 1

The Pain and Power of Stories

Your Story Matters

When I was a little kid, I used to make up stories of who I was going to be when I grew up. I mean, what kid hasn't? But I wouldn't have believed you if you had told me that my life would become a living roller-coaster ride, with steep slopes and quick turns, pain that I would never wish on my worst enemy, and insurmountable suffering. Back then, as I was going through the pain, I would have tried to avoid it all; perhaps I might have even chosen a simpler path with less pain and suffering. Some pains, I chose to bring on myself, while others were thrust upon me and were unavoidable.

I would like to encourage those who are currently experiencing moments of pain and suffering. Your story still matters. It still holds value. Don't ever think for a second that because of the kinds of pain you have gone through or are going through that your story is any less valuable. Don't ever think that that pain or suffering has made you a broken person. Because, my friend, that is simply not true.

One question I ask some of my podcast guests is: if you had another chance at life, what would you do differently? This thought has crossed my mind many times over the years. But I can honestly say, looking back now, that I wouldn't change my path for anything. Not even for all the money in the world. I see my story as valuable because of the pain I have endured. And no monetary amount or the ability to restart my life will ever change that fact for me.

And so today, I *encourage* people to experience and embrace pain, and you'll soon learn all the reasons why.

The Power of Pain

It's sad to think there are people out there who have gone through the unthinkable. Nobody wants to go through pain, yet pain is ultimately an inevitable and unescapable fact of life. Andrew Scipione, the former police commissioner of New South Wales and one of my first guests on *The Story Box*, summed up his experience of pain and suffering in one of the most profound and real definitions I've ever had the privilege of hearing.

He said that nobody wants to see others or their loved ones in tears, or to hear of a traumatic experience that someone endured. For Andrew, pain was an inevitable fact—it was part of being a cop. But as Andrew wisely said, "How you allow the misery to affect you—that's optional. The only person that is going to allow the pain to affect you is you."

He told me a crazy story of arriving on the scene of a serious car crash. The driver was pulled from the car wreck, and Andrew held the man in his arms. He watched as the life went from the man's body, and he realized that once we were gone, there was no physical pain, and this was in fact a gift—for both the deceased and the ones left to carry on. And because of this, we have a choice to allow our existence to be ruined by the painful, traumatic experience or decide to rise above it all and move forward in our lives.

After hearing this, I felt chills run down my spine. I then reflected back on the many pains I had endured and realized that I had wasted my life by letting the pain engulf me for such a long time, and so from that moment on, I chose to continue to rise above my traumas and instead use that pain in my stories to help others who might experience something similar in their own lives.

There is one bird that tries to inflict a great deal of pain on an eagle. As the eagle is flying, the crow will sit on the eagle's back, biting its neck. The eagle doesn't respond or fight the crow, as it doesn't believe in wasting its time or energy on it. The eagle is a wise bird, and instead of wasting time on the pain, the eagle opens its enormous wings and begins to rise higher in the sky.

The higher the eagle climbs, the harder it becomes for the crow to breathe. Eventually, the crow will fall off due to the lack of oxygen.

We waste so much of our time and energy focused on the pain in our lives, which brings us down. When we focus on the *pain* life can bring, that will lead to *suffering*. Stop wasting your time on pain. Be like the eagle when a crow comes to inflict pain—rise higher. Stay true to your path, learn what you need to learn from the pain, and continue to move toward new heights.

The Power of Your Story

Stories have a huge impact on our daily lives. They have the power to connect us all from vast expanses of our world, and yet stories also have the power to disconnect us all too. We currently live in a world where the media plagues our screens with dramatic stories to create tension and, often, to cause fear. That's really a perfect example of how powerful stories are. They dive deep into our psyche, and if we aren't careful, the fear-based stories can control our beliefs on what's real and what's not.

Whether we realize it or not, every one of us is creating stories every day. And while you might not be writing a book about all the stories that you create every day, people are watching your stories—children, in particular.

Think about this for a moment.

It could be that a child might take what they've seen of your story to his/her parent, or share it with their friends on the playground. Your story could either set a good example and create positive change and growth or it could do the opposite.

God gave us an incredible gift called free will—the ability to choose. But with that free will comes consequences: good or bad. I don't know about you, but I want my story to leave a positive ripple effect for not just children, but the whole world, to be inspired by.

What choice will you make?

I know that you haven't read my whole story, but trust me, you can save yourself from a lot of pain if you choose to wisely work toward making a positive difference in the world. The world already has enough negative influences. Why add more?

Be Curious and Learn from Stories

Growing up, I never used to be good at connecting with children my own age. I just didn't seem to get along or relate with any of their stories. I found the adults' stories far more fascinating; I would always hang around people who were older than me. I loved asking them questions and hearing their responses, especially when I found out that I was learning, and boy did I love to learn, as I still do.

I was very much a curious child, always asking questions even if they were sometimes silly. Curiosity never killed anyone important: in fact, it was because they were curious that they became important in the first place.

I enjoyed reading stories of men and women throughout history, such as: Martin Luther King Jr. and Sr.; Muhammad Ali; Abraham Lincoln; Albert Einstein; Thomas Edison; Jesus Christ; John the Baptist; Paul the Apostle; Peter, James, and John; King David; Mary; Mother Teresa; Anne Frank; Corrie Ten Boom; Margaret Thatcher; and Leonardo da Vinci, to name a few. These men and women weren't perfect, except for Jesus—but the others were far from it.

Peter was a curious-minded individual—the story of when he walked on water wasn't just about faith in action, it was also about wanting to know the answer to whether Jesus was actually walking on the water. Because of Peter's curiosity, that story of how he walked on water toward Jesus has been passed down throughout generations.

When you're curious, you never know where you'll end up or what answer will be given. But don't let that stop you from asking a question or taking a step into the unknown!

A huge lesson my grandy taught me was this: *if you don't ask, you don't get.*

He used to drive me home after art lessons, which he graciously gave up his valuable time to take me to, as he said he believed in me and wanted to give me the best experiences possible. We normally stopped on our way home at a gas station, and my grandy would give me money to buy a Magnum ice cream and a killer python snake candy. In those days, you were able to get the giant snakes for only twenty cents. (Which was cheap back then. Nowadays, they rip you off for a small packet of candy [lollies]. Oh, how I miss the old days…sometimes.)

However, when we were on this drive home, my grandy didn't seem to be in a good mood, so we didn't stop at all. I thought it was weird that we didn't stop, but I didn't *ask* him why we didn't stop as per our normal routine.

He could obviously tell I was upset, so he asked me, "What's wrong?"

I responded in a disappointed tone, "We didn't stop for ice cream and my snake."

My grandy looked at me and in his wisdom responded with, "You should have asked me to stop."

Turns out that just because my grandy looked grumpy didn't mean that he wouldn't have stopped.

The point of this story is to illustrate two important lessons.

The first is: if you don't ask, you don't get.

And secondly: never be afraid to ask, for if you don't ask, you'll never know the answer.

If you don't get the response you want, then that's okay! The very worst someone can say is no. Then what? You continue to be curious and find another way. Don't allow fear to control your curiosity. We need more curious-minded people! Curiosity shows a desire to learn and grow. But sadly, with our current world, we're losing our curious minds to fear, which is caused by false information being heavily portrayed on our screens.

According to *New York Times* bestselling author, scientist, and international educator Gregg Braden, there is a battle going on right now for our very humanness. What makes us more human is the ability for us to have the freedom and liberty to be curious. When we cease curiosity, we cease being human. We become robots programmed to do the bidding of our master. How is that *living*?

The Changes in Your Story

Ever since I was eight years old, my dream was to become a famous filmmaker and storyteller. And not only did I look up to men such as Steven Spielberg, but I also looked up to my uncle Paul, because he was a filmmaker and a lover of stories too—especially the good ones!

I loved hearing all the stories about Uncle Paul being on set for major Hollywood blockbusters, which made me want to grow up fast so that I could be on a filmset with him. Uncle Paul even met my idol, Steven Spielberg, and so I said to myself as a young boy: *one day I'm going to meet that man and hear his stories in person.*

Today, as I am writing this at twenty-four years of age, I still have that same dream and goal of meeting Steven Spielberg.

The twelve months leading up to my high school graduation, I wanted to attend film school; however, I was advised by the people I love and respected, including Uncle Paul, that going to film school was not the best path to take at that time. I really struggled with this advice, especially when Uncle Paul advised me against going after my goal.

Being a filmmaker was my dream, and film school seemed like the obvious path to take...right? Well, no—I was the one who thought he knew best, and when I look back on that period of my life, I'm grateful that I listened to the advice from those close to me.

Writing this part of my story makes me cringe at how naive, proud, and egocentric I was back then. I thought I knew what was best for my life. After the door to becoming a filmmaker was closed, or so I thought, I had a crazy idea that maybe becoming a nurse would be a wise option.

My gracious mom took me to the open day of one college that offered a degree in nursing, and we did the tour, but something inside me didn't feel right. About a week later, I changed my mind again. This time though, it was business college.

I inquired about a business college near our home and instantly loved the environment and people. On the open day, I wanted to sign up and would have been accepted. However, Mom advised me strongly to at least complete high school and get my HSC (High School Certificate, which basically tells you that you've finished school and whether you are "smart" enough to get into a university or not), and then if I was still interested, attend business college. I'm thankful that I listened to her advice again, despite the struggle it was to complete that year.

One of the main reasons I wanted to go was because of one man. He was famous among the alumni—they all respected and looked up to him. When I first met him, I shook his hand and the only thing he said to me was, "You are going to be successful one day." That was it, then he went back and kept teaching his class.

I found out later that he had never said that to any other student—yet he was saying it to me, and I wasn't even a student. My mind was instantly buzzing about what I thought real success was: the expensive cars, houses, yachts...you know, all the cliché items/possessions we are conditioned to believe successful people have, which can still be true for many people. And let me say that having all the above is not a bad thing. It's just a very shallow way of looking at *success*.

I eventually studied at this business college, and I found myself in a whole new world. It was completely different than the environment I was used to for the past thirteen years of my life. My entire routine was shaken, and it felt like I was starting all over again, from making new friends to studying harder and allocating more time to my assignments. I was excited at first because it was all new, and I was keen to be under the tutelage of the same teacher who had told me that I was going to be successful one day.

He recognized me when I walked into his classroom and gave me an acknowledging nod. I was pleased to be in his class. I was the first one to sit down at the back of the classroom, and I was wearing a fresh blue suit.

My teacher looked at me and asked for my name.

I replied, "It's Jarred Fantom, sir."

He nodded, was quiet for a moment, and then repeated the same phrase he had told me a year earlier. But this time, though it carried more weight behind it as he was now using my name, he said, "Jarred, there is something different about you. I know that you are going to be successful one day."

Before I could say anything, all the other students started piling in and taking their seats. Once everyone had been seated, we went around the room introducing ourselves to one another. My teacher never said to any of the other students that they would be successful, just to me, which I thought was very strange.

One afternoon, I chose to stay back after class to complete an assignment when all the other students had gone home. My teacher had packed up his stuff and was closing up his class-room when he noticed me sitting outside the classroom at a table doing my work. He walked over and said, "Jarred, you are going to be successful one day. Keep going." And then he walked away.

I felt goose bumps all over my body when he said that for the *third* time. This man had achieved great success in busi-ness, and he had earned millions in the process. So of course I thought that's what he meant when he kept telling me I would be successful one day. He didn't have to teach our class; in fact, he traveled on a train three days of the week for four hours just to teach us. Knowing this made me respect the man even more and trust his opinion.

The first semester, I was enthusiastic about being there. It was new and exciting. I was even voted the class president, along with another student. We'd oversee events, fundraisers, birthdays, and if anyone wanted to share suggestions, we'd hold a weekly meeting.

One Wednesday morning during the end of the first semester, I was about to take a very important exam. This exam was made out to be the "most important exam of the year." You know, the ones that are always hyped up so that you study more. To be honest, I didn't study for this exam. I thought that I knew all the content already and the exam would be a breeze. It's funny because I wasn't great at exams; in fact, in eleventh grade, I suffered a massive panic attack before my HSC trial exams. So why I thought I didn't need to study is beyond me.

The time to take the exam arrived, and we all took our seats. I was a little nervous, mainly because I knew this exam was important and I hadn't prepared for it at all. My teacher walked in and asked the class if we had any questions before we started.

No one put up their hand. So, I thought I would be smart and ask a question, thinking that I'd get an answer relating to the exam itself. I asked if he had any advice for us in taking this test.

He calmly looked at me as if he knew I wasn't prepared for the exam. He paused for a few moments and then proceeded to tell this powerful story...

> High up in the Himalayan mountains lived a wise old man. Periodically, the wise old man ventured down to the local village. The villagers all went up to the wise old man and

asked him questions, which the wise old man always answered correctly.

One day, a group of boys decided to play a trick on the wise old man. They thought they could prove that he was a fraud. So, they devised a cunning plan—they would catch a bird, walk up to the wise old man and ask, "Old man, old man, what do I have in my hands?" If the wise old man said it was a bird, then they would ask if the bird was alive or dead. If the wise old man answered it was alive, then the boys would crush the bird, killing it. But if the wise old man answered it was dead, the boys would free the bird. Thus, no matter what the answer was, they would prove that the wise old man was a fraud.

The day came when the wise old man came back to the village. The young boys quickly caught a bird and went straight to the wise old man.

Sure enough, one of the boys asked, "Old man, old man, what do I have in my hands?"

The wise old man looked at the boy and said, "You have a bird, my son."

The boy holding the bird replied, "That is correct, but is it alive or is it dead?"

The wise old man thought for a moment and looked into the young boy's eyes. He responded with, "The choice whether that bird lives or dies is up to you, my son."

Here is the moral of that story: we all have a choice in life, and whatever choice we decide to make, we need to learn to live with the results of that choice, whether good or bad.

This lesson still holds true to my life today. I have told this same story to countless people. It's a powerful reminder for all of us to understand that we have been given an amazing gift called life. And that we should always value and be mindful of the choices that we make every day, as they form the degree in which change happens.

This wasn't exactly the kind of advice I was hoping to hear from my teacher. Needless to say, after that experience, I made the choice to study for my future exams, even though studying for exams wasn't my strong suit.

During the middle of the second semester, the teacher I had admired left. I also noticed similarities in my coursework to twelfth grade business studies. So, my attitude shifted, and I rebelled for the first time ever in a school-like environment. I stopped wearing suits to class. I didn't hang out with anyone and kept mostly to myself during the short fifteen- to twenty-minute meal break between classes and lunch. I would get my work done well in advance so I could leave early to go to the gym. I complained to my parents about wanting to leave my college, as I wasn't happy there anymore.

However, I couldn't ignore my grandy's wise words that kept coming to mind every time I wanted to quit: "Jarred, if you start something, make sure you finish strong. Giving up is easy but sticking through until the end is more worthwhile. Great leaders are born through the tough times."

So I persisted, but my heart still wasn't in it.

The teachers soon saw my change in attitude, and they constantly judged me for losing the passion I had in my first semester. Truth be told, I simply wasn't inspired or happy with where I was anymore. As much as I wanted to simply leave, I still honored my parents' wishes and kept at it for the whole year until graduation, although my attitude while I was there wasn't great. I still graduated with honors, and I have no idea how I managed to do that.

Even though I thought these experiences were painful, they taught me several important lessons.

The first being: change will happen in life; we just need to embrace the change. And the choice of how you react to the change is up to you.

The second is: success is relative to you and looking at "stuff" as success is just a shallow and unfulfilling approach to real success.

The third and final thing that I learned is: despite the pain and power of your story, and no matter how often it changes, it's a gift to be cherished and valued!

Believe in Your Story

A gentleman was walking through an elephant camp one day when he spotted an elephant not being kept in any cage or by chains. The man looked at the elephant more closely and discovered that the elephant was being held by a small piece of rope tied to one of its legs. The man was confused by this. He couldn't understand why the elephant wouldn't just use his great strength to break free and escape.

Wanting to know the answer to this confusion, he asked the trainer why the elephant didn't escape.

The trainer replied, "When the elephants are very young and much smaller, we use the same size rope to tie them, and at that age, it's enough to hold them. As they grow up, they're conditioned to believe they can't break away. They believe the rope can still hold them, so they never try to break free."

The moral of that story is that no matter how much society will try and hold you back, always continue to believe that if you want it bad enough, anything is possible. Believing you can is the most important step in one day achieving it.

Belief is a powerful motivator—it can and will propel you forward if you choose it. For many years, I didn't believe in the power of my story. I allowed negative influences and false conditioned beliefs to cloud all my perceptions of myself. Like the elephant, I got stuck, thinking that my story wasn't valuable to anyone. And that simply wasn't true at all.

Those false, conditioned beliefs were only lies.

The sadder truth for many people is that they don't even know they have a rope attached to them. The conditioned belief is so bad that they feel they can't move forward, so they just stay.

You can break free—that choice is yours, and yours alone.

I'm here today to tell you that *your story matters*!

It's time you start believing that it's worth more than gold, and start telling yourself this frequently.

You will *almost* definitely believe what you tell yourself daily. The reason why I say "almost" is because you can choose at any moment to stop what you tell yourself. You can change, so why not now?

I'll finish this chapter with a simple thought.

We may never know the impact that our stories can have on someone. Knowing this truth should encourage us even more to share our stories. Just think: your story could be the inspiration or motivation that someone needs in their life right now. You may never receive the applause or even a thank you, but that doesn't and shouldn't matter.

Believe me, I understand that some stories might be too personal and heartbreaking to share. If you aren't comfortable, that's okay. Always remember, though, if you can potentially motivate, inspire, challenge, educate, or even help a person transform in a positive way with your story, why hold back?

CHAPTER 2

The Birth of an Eagle

Starting Is Only Just Half the Battle

My name is Jarred Paul Fantom, but most people call me Jay. Why? Well, I've had a lot of people spell and say my name wrong. So, I thought it would be easier for people to call me "Jay" instead. I was born in Westmead Hospital, Sydney, Australia, on the twenty-ninth day of some month I won't disclose.

Apparently, I entered the world with a huge smile on my face. I always like to tell people that—I was either happy to be out of the darkness, or I wanted to try and make this dark world a brighter place. I'll let you decide which option you want to believe. The nurses said they had never seen a baby born with such a wide smile before. It was clear to my parents and the nurses that I was a "special child," or that's what I like to say at least.

Mom has recounted a few stories of my initial years, saying that while my brothers and I were all born unique and individual blessings, I seemed to come with many health issues that were well outside of the normal medical textbook. You could honestly write an actual medical textbook on some of my health cases, as there are so many strange and unexplained ones. Spending time in and out of the Westmead Children's Hospital was the norm for my childhood.

I was born with severe gastric reflux, a gene that was also passed onto my two brothers. It affected us in different ways. Mom and Dad certainly had their work cut out for them in knowing how to manage it and reduce the symptoms and severe pain that came along with it. Out of all three of us boys, my symptoms were easiest to detect in the tests, which was quite rare.

At six months old, I became very unwell with high fevers and just feeling out of sorts. Mom took me to the GP, who put it down to teething. However, my mom wasn't convinced.

This doctor was still unsure what was wrong with me even after seeing me a few times, and so my mom asked him if it could be a urinary tract infection. Now, my mom had never heard of a baby getting a UTI, nor had she had much prior knowledge of how to deal with it either, but for some reason it just came to her mind. The doctor agreed that there was a high chance of it being a UTI, and he did some tests.

The tests came back saying that I had blood in my urine and high protein levels, which indicated a nasty infection. And not only that, but it seemed as if this wasn't the first infection I had, and even more concerning was that there was scarring to my right kidney.

I was also diagnosed with kidney reflux, and the specialist that was looking after me said that there was no need for surgery. I was tested every week for the first twelve months of my life, and then once a month I was given antibiotics when needed.

When I was twelve years old, I had some very bad and unusual kidney pain. We also discovered that my creatine levels were high and had been for months. I was once again taken back to the Westmead Children's Hospital, which became my home away from home from then on.

This time, however, I was admitted to the renal ward. I saw children my age and older on dialysis and on waiting lists for kidney transplants. It was sad to see these beautiful people suffering so much.

So I saw this as a perfect opportunity to try and make the patients laugh. Around the same time, I met this awesome nephrologist, who looked after me until I became an adult.

Dr. Steve, as he loved to be called, told my parents that it was not normal for a baby or child to have UTI infections unless there was an underlying bladder or kidney issue. So I went to see Dr. Steve quite a few times before he finally decided to do a kidney biopsy to rule out nephritis. Nephritis is a condition in which the functional units of the kidneys become inflamed and thus affect the kidneys' ability to function.

I'll try to explain the feeling after having a kidney biopsy. It's not fun at all! You can hardly move without this sharp piercing pain in your side. Laughing doesn't help either, and don't get me started on the pain experienced before, while, and after you pee.

Thank the Lord the results came back negative, but I was still in danger of developing nephritis at any time of my life. This meant that the way I chose to live my life needed to be based on mindfully protecting my kidneys. To this day, I've never touched a drop of alcohol or smoked a cigarette. I don't drink soft drinks at all, and I can't have a great deal of protein either. I'm grateful, though, for this lifestyle. It's not a weakness to have this kidney problem—it's the complete opposite. In fact, it's been more of a strength to me over the years. I've never known what it's like to feel so drunk that I can't feel my face or not remember the night before.

Every year I go and see an adult nephrologist who monitors my kidney function. He has told me that eventually, I may need to have a kidney transplant. Although I'm mindful of this, it doesn't worry me because I know that God has everything under control.

An eagle's start is not easier either. A wedge-tailed eagle, which is twice the size of an American eagle, lays two to three eggs a year, and each egg is laid two to four days apart. The first egg has a higher chance of survival than the other eggs, as it usually hatches first. The second eaglet that hatches must fight for survival.

That's what I had to do when I was born—fight for my own survival.

I was born into a very conservative Christian household. My mom placed her faith in Jesus Christ before she met my dad. She had decided not to marry a non-Christian man, as she had had three broken engagements before my dad came along. They met at a gym; my dad was the one who made first contact, and Mom shared the gospel straight away with him and invited him to church. As my dad wasn't saved at the time, the only way he could get to know my mom further was to go to her church. So, he went, and after a few months, he eventually trusted Christ as his savior. My parents began dating not long after that. When my dad met my grandmother, she instantly liked him.

She shared this story. My grandmother needed help pushing the trash in the garbage can down, as it was too high for her to reach and push down. My dad got up on the bin and crushed all the trash down for her. What a gentleman, right? My grandy, on the other hand, wasn't so easily convinced or won over. However, my dad was still determined to be the best for my mom.

My grandy gave my dad a hard time, as you can imagine, especially when Dad asked Grandy for Mom's hand in marriage. The way my dad described it: "Jarred, it was a long—a very long and hard—conversation."

And I believe him because one thing I'll tell you about my grandy is that that man knew how to get his point across.

My mom had always desired to become a mother. However, she was told by doctors that because of what she had done to her body earlier in life, she wouldn't be able to have children. Mum also had thyroid disease and polycystic ovary syndrome or PCOS for short. But Mom kept praying and made a promise to God very much like Hannah in the book of 1 Samuel—that if she had a baby, then she would always take care of her body and raise her children to serve God.

Well, God honored that prayer, and despite the doctor's diagnosis, Mom became pregnant with my older brother Nathan. When my mom was six months pregnant, my dad's father was diagnosed with stage four pancreatic cancer. The surgeons were unable to save him, and he sadly passed away six days before Nathan was born. All within one week, Mom and Dad had a death, funeral, birth, and wedding anniversary.

Nathan was about twenty months old when Mom became pregnant again, but this time the pregnancy was very different, and Mom sensed that something wasn't right. When she was checked by her obstetrician, he confirmed that Mom had lost the baby. This was devastating news for my parents; however, they continued to trust in God, knowing that he promises to comfort those who need comforting. Mom kept being faithful, praying to God for another child, and six months later, she became pregnant with me. I like to boast about the fact that out of my brothers, I was the "planned one."

Life in the Fantom household wasn't exactly easy early on. At times, my dad had to work two to three jobs just to put food on the table. He was a hard worker and did what he could. We always had what we needed and never went without the essentials. Since my dad was away most of the time working, it meant that Mom was doing most of the teaching and discipline. I can say a lot about my mom, but she is the kindest, most loving, most caring, most faithful, and strongest woman that I know, who gives up so much of her time and energy for her family. I wouldn't be the man I am today without my mom, and I'll never be able to thank her for that.

We were raised with good values, many of which I have kept over the years. One important value was toward having an excellent spirit about whatever we did. I used to go over to my grandparents' place to mow their lawn, and if I had a good attitude then I received pocket money.

My grandy didn't have to give us money for doing his lawn, and I certainly didn't expect it, but he wanted to instill in us the mindset of receiving a reward when you did an excellent job, while also having an excellent spirit. He wanted to make sure we were raised with the right work ethic and good values as well.

This one time, I was tired—and when I get tired, I get angry and frustrated sometimes, especially when I don't want to do something. I really didn't want to mow the lawn that day and threw the biggest tantrum. Needless to say, I didn't get any money. However, I was disciplined God's way, and I still had to mow the lawn, only this time I had to do my section and my older brother's section too.

After I had finished both lawns, I asked Grandy for my twenty dollars. He looked at me and—again in his wisdom—said, "I don't reward bad attitudes. I reward excellent attitudes."

I quickly realized that having an excellent spirit and attitude about whatever I was doing was by far the better choice.

Mom had her convictions on how to raise us boys from the Bible and she did her best to do so. At times it seemed controlling, protective, and overly conservative to the outside world. I didn't miss out on much though; Mom always made sure we had a great understanding of rules, discipline, right from wrong, and how to respect and treat people. Even though we weren't allowed to do many things growing up—like go to the movies or watch films that were over PG-13 in rating— looking back now, it didn't really matter because some of the greatest stories can be found in books.

I grew up with all the classic stories, such as *Charlotte's Web, Uncle Tom's Cabin, Rikki Tikki Tavi, Robinson Crusoe, The Swiss Family Robinson, Old Yeller*, "Jack and the Beanstalk," "David and Goliath," "Samson and Delilah," and that of Jesus Christ, to name a few. And it was these stories, among many others, that helped shape my understanding of the world and how people behave.

Having a conservative outlook on life did shape my identity growing up. The sad truth is that many children growing up in conservative households with these restrictions tend to eventually walk away from it all after the "veil" is removed from their eyes. I'm guilty of doing that for a period of time.

I have never liked the party or clubbing scene and felt like it was a massive waste of my precious time. I'm very much an introverted individual, which means that I tend to stay away from large and loud environments as much as possible. This is just my opinion, but I never found clubs to be fun or my idea of a good time. I'd much rather stay home, read a good book, watch a movie, or be in silence away from all the noise of the world. I love to think, and I find that noise tends to distract me from my creativity.

For a while, I was convinced that I didn't need to go to heaven. I guess you could say that I was stubborn. One night, when I was six years old, Mom was reading a devotional about an old man who was dying, and he didn't know if he was going to heaven or not. I was sitting next to Mom, then suddenly, I pushed the book out of Mom's hand and sat on her lap facing her and said with my hands on my hips, "Mommy, I'm ready to go to heaven now."

My mom explained what Jesus had done for me by dying on the cross for the sins of the whole world. I asked God to forgive me of my sins and to come into my heart and save me. From then on, I became a child of God. When I turned ten, I made another statement of faith just to make sure.

I didn't start going to school until I was five and a half years old. This was due to a few reasons: I wasn't exactly the sharpest tool in the shed. I struggled to focus on schoolwork, as my mind was always on other things. (My dad used to call it "being off with the fairies"). And I had learning difficulties early on.

So Mom made the decision to homeschool me, as I was very immature and struggled to interact with younger children. I enjoyed the company of older people more than I did children my own age. However, I do realize that it must have driven them crazy with the number of ridiculous questions I used to ask them. Like I mentioned in the earlier chapter, I was a curious kid.

My parents had been praying for a school to send us boys to for a while. The Lord eventually directed them to a school that was about to open. In faith, Mom and Dad put their names down and paid a small fee to hold Nathan's place. We were the first family to sign up to this school, which is a bit of history for you. It was literally in the middle of nowhere, surrounded by farms, chickens, cows, sheep, and a lot of foliage. You could always tell if you were close or not because of the smell. It was only a small school; I don't even remember how many children there were at the start.

Let me just say that I was never the brightest kid during my time at school. It was quite evident early on that I struggled with English, math, science…pretty much every subject, really. However, I seemed to love the creative writing part of English. I would get so excited when my teacher announced it was time to write a story. Sheer joy virtually expelled from me! During this time, I could let my brain run wild; I felt like this was what I was meant to be doing.

I used to create the most outrageous stories that my teachers sometimes couldn't believe I wrote. I realized during this time that despite everything that was going on around me, I had the power to create whatever I wanted to, and the only limits were the time I had in class and my own imagination. As I mentioned earlier, I've never been great at grammar. Imagine I'm Batman and grammar is the Joker. We are worst enemies, and yet we're symbiotic—without the Joker, Batman wouldn't be Batman.

But never allow a weakness to stop you from doing something you want to do.

I was bullied in elementary and high school. In elementary school, I was called a "class snitch," and of course no one likes a snitch. This seemed to make me more enemies than friends. But more than that, I was bullied because I was "different." And people are often afraid of what is different. There was this one girl who really had it out for me. She'd tease me often about my looks and followed me wherever I went, basically harassing the living daylights out of me. It made me hate going to school. I dreaded every single moment of class. If you have ever been bullied, you know the pain that I'm describing.

I always complained to Mom when we were driving home from school or even on the way to school. Mom took a loving and caring approach toward the bullying, and she often spoke about the issue to the school principal. When I look back on it now, this whole experience was teaching me resilience and grit, and how to handle bullying the right way.

Eventually, the girl left the school, and I had to transition into high school where I was yet again bullied by another kid. But instead of verbal abuse, he abused me physically and verbally. One day I was standing by myself minding my own business near the basketball courts, just watching everyone play, when suddenly, the bully jumped on my back. I wasn't strong enough to support his weight, and three of my ribs popped out in succession. The pain was so bad that it was hard for me to move or stand up straight.

The pain lasted for a few weeks before I finally went to see a musculoskeletal specialist who temporarily fixed the problem. However, because of that incident, I have constant back pain, and I still need to sometimes see the specialist every so often to put me back into place. Today, I need to exercise to maintain strength in those areas.

Eventually, I got fed up with being bullied by this kid, so I took matters into my own hands. During lunch one afternoon, the bully tried picking on me again in front of everyone. But this time I said, "Stop it or else." (You know, the classic line you say to get people to leave you alone.)

He replied, "You can't hurt me."

Well, in front of the whole school, (which wasn't many students) I picked up this bully (I honestly don't know how I managed to do that as he was double my size!) and slammed him into the ground. I then said, "Don't you ever touch me again."

The children watching all looked shocked, but they started clapping. This situation didn't solve or help the problem though. In fact, it only amplified it.

That was the first and only fight I ever got into at school. I decided not to fight with him again, as it just wasn't worth it, and I didn't see it doing any good anyway. He did try several times after that incident to get back at me. But this time I just walked away.

Bullying is never acceptable. Period. Today, I'm passionate about spreading awareness on this issue to help combat the problem. Children today aren't just facing bullying in person at school; they're facing it each time they log onto social media. Parents, do you know what your children are looking at on social media? Do you know how your children are feeling mentally? They might not want to share out of fear.

And young people, if you are being bullied, don't ever be afraid to speak up about it. Your mental health is so precious that it must be valued at all costs. Don't allow someone online or in person threaten your mental health. You have the power to rise above it.

Parents, help your children as best you can—I implore you. They're living through some of the worse times imaginable.

What I did to cope with the bullying was read books. There is an old truth that says that "readers are leaders." It's because the more you read, the more knowledge you gain, and as a result, the more mature your brain becomes.

Books hold timeless wisdom, and if you want to become a great leader someday, then absorb all the knowledge from leaders who have written everything down for you in a book. Even today, that saying holds its power.

Knowledge is the embodiment of power, and the more you read, the more powerful you become. A good leader is one who reads and puts into practice what they are reading. Reading helped take me out of the negative world that I felt surrounded me and it transported me into a new world filled with endless possibilities, newfound wisdom, and valuable insights.

I also took solace and found safety with good stories. Stories were a fantastic source of emotional escape. Reading good books gave me most of the answers I was seeking to help me combat the bullying. The many books I read all spoke about how it was better to just walk away from a fight than get into one. I know as men we have that desire to show our masculine side, especially if we're being abused; however, I never found it satisfying to fight back with my fists. Even after I slammed that bully into the ground at my school. I realize now that I could have handled that whole situation a lot better and avoided using violence toward him.

To fight a bully, one must learn to forgive constantly, turn the other cheek, and then go seek help. There is no need for violence. And violence never solves anything anyway. It just creates more problems, as I found out. There is great wisdom in this, and it doesn't come from me, but from God. It was God who said to forgive those that hurt you and do good to them that despise you.

Easier said than done, right? But again, we all have a choice to work at it. And believe me, it's far better than the alternative.

Why People Hate

Like bullying, hate is a vile and vicious disease that sadly plagues much of our world today. Instead of loving one another and accepting people for the way they are, we (including me) judge, ridicule, and make people feel worthless. Why?

Well, let me share a story to delve deeper into this question…

A seven-year-old African American boy asked his mother one day. "Momma, why do people hate?"

With sad eyes, the boy's mom looked down at her young son and replied, "Son, there are two reasons for why people hate. The first is: people hate what they don't understand."

The young boy quickly yelled, "Well, I hate not understanding."

The boy's mother paused for a moment. She shook her head and replied, "The second reason why people hate is because they have chosen to hate. You see, son, it is a choice to hate someone else. Loving another human is hard work, which is why not many people choose love. I want you to know that the difference between a boy and a man is that a boy chooses to follow others that hate even when he doesn't fully understand why in the first place. A man seeks out the truth; he isn't quick to judge; he does the hard work, and he persistently and unconditionally loves despite the challenges that may face him. So, son, what are you going to be? A boy or a man?"

The little boy, without even having to think, responded with four simple yet powerful words: "Momma, I choose love."

That answer was all the boy's mother needed to hear to know that her son understood what she had just said.

A few years later, that boy's mother was taken from him in a horrendous display of hatred that no one from the town had ever witnessed before. The boy was only ten years old at the time and on his way home from school. He arrived home to see police cars and ambulances surrounding his house. The young boy was scared and quickly rushed toward his house.

Fear began to set in as the young boy reached the men in blue uniforms.

One of the officers noticed the little boy's face and quickly made the assessment that he was the son. He picked up the stressed young boy, and walked him away from the house. The officer then kneeled to the young boy's level and looked him in the eyes. "I'm sorry, son, but your momma is gone. I'm so sorry."

The young boy broke down in tears; complete shock had taken over his system. He collapsed into the officer's arms. The white man who committed the murder was sentenced to forty years behind bars without parole.

The young boy, now a young man, had spent many years trying to understand why his mother was taken from him. Why this man could have done what he did. He hated the man for what he did. One day, the young man decided to go and see the murderer in prison. He wanted to know why this random white man murdered his precious and innocent mother for what seemed like to the young man, no reason at all.

As the murderer walked into the visiting room, the young man saw that years in prison hadn't been kind to this person. He was a small, skeleton-like pale human that looked like he hadn't shaved in thirteen years. The young man's mind and heart began racing. The visiting area was an open space where there was nowhere to hide. And nowhere to run.

The murderer took a seat, and neither of them said a word for five minutes. They just looked at each other.

Finally, the murderer broke the silence. "I'm not sorry for what I did. She deserved it."

The young man was filled with so much hatred and rage that all he wanted to do was lean over that table and take the murderer's life as payback. But something amazing happened in that moment. It was like a light bulb finally went off in the young man's mind. He remembered when his mother had explained why people hate. It made more sense to him now than it did back then. He remembered that he was going to choose love no matter what. Even though he didn't fully understand why this man hated his mother, apart from the color of her skin. The young man decided to make a life changing choice in that moment.

The young man looks at the murderer dead in his dark brown eyes and replies, "You know, when I came here today, all I could think about was all the things I would say and do to you when I saw you. To be honest, I wanted to kill you. For so many years, I wanted you dead. But hearing you say that you aren't sorry for what you did made me realize something. I spent so much of my life hating you for what you took from me. It was all I could think about most days. My mother said to me once that people hate what they don't understand, and I had chosen to hate not just you but the fact I couldn't understand why you did what you did. Now I understand. And I don't care if you are sorry or not. I choose to forgive and love you anyway, not for your satisfaction but for my own. I choose to forgive and love myself for not doing this sooner. The real prison isn't behind four concrete walls; it's what we say to ourselves and believe in our minds, choosing to hate and not loving or forgiving is the worse prison of them all." With that, the young man decided to do the unthinkable. He reached out to shake the hand of the man who took his mother's life. The same hands that had his mother's blood on them years earlier. Without uttering a word in reply, the murderer slowly lifted his handcuffed hands out from underneath the steel table and extended them to shake the young man's right hand.

After the young man had shaken the murder's hand, he stood up, having said what he needed to say. And he walked out of the prison feeling at peace.

I use this story as a way of illustrating what happens because of hate and what happens when you choose not to hate. The truth is that when we hate, all we are doing is spreading the vile disease and causing more harm to ourselves than anyone else. Can you imagine a world where everyone just chose to *love* rather than to *hate*? Can you imagine a world where people weren't judged by how they look, or what color they are? This was Martin Luther King Jr.'s dream many years ago. Why can't it be all of ours too? Imagine what kind of a world would that be! There would be peace, kindness, prosperity, and growth. Sadly, though, choosing to love someone requires hard work, especially when they caused you pain. And not many people, including myself at times, want to work at what is hard.

When a crow comes to cause an eagle pain, an eagle just chooses to sore higher and keeps its cool despite the pain and pressure.

People should know that they have a choice, and if they aren't afraid to do the hard work on a continual basis as forgiveness, love, respect, and kindness can be ongoing struggles along your journal of life. However, all that daily hard work will eventually lead you to finding peace and harmony within yourself, life, and with others too.

The ultimate example of love is when Jesus willingly made the choice to come down to this earth, live a sinless life, be tempted, and have people spit and throw rocks and chant racist and vile remarks at him. We were all responsible for putting him to death on that cross. My sins, as well as the sins of the entire world, put him there.

It was Jesus' love for us all that kept him there, enduring the worst pain. And all while listening to false accusations being yelled at him.

So why did he choose this?

Because he chose to leave behind the example of *true love* and show us that hate only destroys.

He chose to show us that *love* truly conquers all. It was love that made a way for us to live forever one day. Imagine if God didn't choose to love us all first, even when we hated him.

Fighting the Fear and Doing It Anyway...

The start for an eagle's life is incredibly tough, and starting the process of writing this book was extremely difficult for me. For many months, I contemplated what I was even going to say. At times I was so hard on myself, and I hated my writing, I would delete entire chapters, and I even stopped writing for a while.

This book stayed on my laptop for several months, just waiting for me to find some courage and stop hating myself, to just write what was in my heart and mind. I was so afraid that no one would even want to read the story of a twenty-four-year-old—I mean, have I even lived enough life yet? This was just one of many negative questions and lies that I wrestled with for many months.

Just like hating others, we often hate ourselves and let our negative thoughts hold us back from accomplishing our full potential. And why is this?

I once had a conversation with Josh Kaufman, the author of *How to Fight a Hydra*. The book speaks about how we can "face our fears, pursue our ambitions, and become the heroes we were destined to be." It's such a profound story, and I encourage everyone to read it. Josh really helped me understand that even the best writers struggle at times, and that just like them, I needed to face and defeat the ever-growing "hydra" of fear.

A hydra is a mythical creature that has several heads and was often mentioned in ancient Greek mythology. When the great Hercules fought the hydra, he cut off one of hydra's heads, but two more appeared. Not willing to give up, Hercules then took a flaming torch to scorch each of the necks when he managed to cut off the heads, stopping them from growing back. And that's how he defeated the hydra.

That was what I needed to do with my fear! Face it head-on a bit more *creatively* and with the fire of courage and the will to just do it.

Speaking with Josh was the catalyst for me to figure out the kind of story I really needed to share with the world.

And the more I dove deeper into my story, faced my fears, and learned to defeat them, I realized that my life story and the lessons that I learned along the way have granted me the ability to soar higher in life every time...like an eagle.

This path that I'm on that God has so wisely gifted and blessed me with may have its ups and downs, wild challenges, fears, insecurities, and numerous failures, but I know I'm on the best path possible now—the path of an eagle.

I put my hope, trust, and all that I am in the belief that when I am weak, the Lord will renew my strength. I can then soar high like an eagle; I can run and not get tired; I can walk down this path for however long God allows me to, and I can always give my very best.

That's enough for me.

CHAPTER 3

Let Challenges Serve You

Don't Give Up Just Because You Face Adversity

Challenges will either make or break you. Challenges come and go in our lives; what defines you through challenges is your attitude during them, not the challenge itself. The weight and pressure may seem like too much to handle at times, so you may feel like giving up—because giving up is easy.

There have been many times when I said to myself, *I'm done. I can't do this anymore. Life is too hard.* But I want to encourage people to take on the challenges that life has to offer. You will become stronger and wiser because of going through them. Life will also offer you short cuts, or "easy paths." However, these paths will never be as fulfilling as the challenging paths.

Don't ever give up!

Imagine that there are two people with two totally different mindsets about to climb a mountain.

The first person's mindset is one of growth. They don't mind hardship because they know that through hardship there will be growth, improvement, and then ultimately success.

The second person doesn't have a growth mindset at all. In fact, they hate challenges so much that they choose to avoid them at all costs. They just want a comfortable life without pain at all. (How many of you can relate to the second person?)

There are only two paths to the top of this mountain.

The first path is the hardest and most challenging—it's the path that takes the most amount of time, it causes more struggle and anguish, and it inflicts the most pain.

The second path is a direct and easy route straight to the top—there is no challenge at all; in fact, it's so easy that you could do the climb three times and still manage to beat the person who took the first path.

The first person walks up to the base of the mountain and looks at the first path. They notice that the first path is the most difficult, and the most challenging. Then they look at the second path and notice how easy it is. The first person decides that they are going to take the first path, and so they begin their climb.

The second person walks up to the base of the mountain not long after the first person left to begin their climb. They notice that the first person is already struggling. Their mind immediately goes into flight mode to avoid any kind of pain. The moment the second person notices the second path and how easy it is, they decide to take that path instead.

Which person do you think took the right path?

What path would you take?

The truth is that it's a matter of perspective and how we see challenges. Do we want to embrace them or run away from them? Sometimes you don't have a choice. But like I mentioned earlier, what defines you through those challenges is your *attitude*.

The second person reaches the top of the mountain first. They don't feel any different than when they started the climb.

So, they decide to climb it again. Once they reach the top for a second time, they still don't feel any different. So, they decide to climb it again. The moment the second person reaches the top of the mountain for a third and final time, they still can't figure out why they feel the same as when they first started the climb. They decide to wait until the first person reaches the top and then ask them a few questions.

When the first person reaches the top of the mountain hours later, they are bruised, battered, and bleeding. The first person then looks back at what they just climbed. They may feel tired, they may be bleeding, but they are fulfilled with the fact that they didn't give up when it got tough. They smile, as now they realize that they are stronger, and they've learned not to give up despite the challenges. Their attitude is positive.

The second person asks the first, "Why are you smiling?"

The first person replies, "Look at what I just climbed. I did that and I didn't give up even when it was hard."

You see, the second person may have taken the easy road, but once they reached the top for a third time, they still felt unhappy and unfulfilled because there were no challenges; they didn't grow, improve, or get stronger, and they remained the same.

The first person, despite going through some incredible challenges, felt fulfilled by what they had achieved.

In life, many want to take the easy path to the top. But when you finally reach the top after you've taken shortcut after shortcut, the top won't seem as grand as what you originally thought it would be.

I don't want to be like the second person with a mindset of no growth.

We were created to move forward in our lives, to thrive and to constantly improve. God created a wonderful thing that through challenges we become stronger, we grow, and we learn.

Without challenges, we would remain the same person physically, spiritually, and mentally. Let the challenges serve you, not the other way around.

When we *serve* the challenges, we open ourselves up to far greater pain than if we were to allow challenges to serve us instead. Don't fight challenges—the more you fight them, the more you get hurt. Instead, embrace them with open arms, hearts, and minds. Because that's when you allow your challenge to serve you and your growth.

Always remember that you can choose to become a victim of the pain and challenges that you are facing, or you can become a victor and conquer life...just like the eagle.

The Challenges of Loss and Grief

The Fantom family is a German Shepherd-or-nothing kind of family. Ever since I was little, I was surrounded by our family German Shepherd called Missy. She was a beautiful, loving, and caring dog. She was also well trained by my dad. We all loved her dearly. German Shepherds are very intelligent dogs.

When my mom was thirty-seven weeks pregnant with my younger brother Jonny, the doctors were concerned about the lack of growth since six months gestation. They told her that they needed to induce her and deliver Jonny early, as they were worried for Jonny's safety.

Mom decided to have an independent ultrasound, which wasn't conclusive. On the same day, Missy's behavior changed, and she wouldn't leave Mom alone and kept nudging Mom in the stomach and smelling her. She then went on a hunger strike and refused to eat for days and seemed quite anxious. Mom went into hospital on the Thursday morning to have Jonny induced.

When he was born, the doctors were amazed he was still alive because there was no blood or life in the placenta; it had been calcifying and deteriorating for months. The doctors told my parents he should have been stillborn. It was only by the grace of God that he wasn't, and Missy knew there was something wrong all along.

Dad went home that night and told Missy that Mom and Jonny were okay, and she finally ate her dinner and seemed happy.

A few years later, when Missy was nine, we had a normal day: we played with her, she had dinner, then we put her outside in her kennel to sleep. The next morning, I woke to hear Mom screaming. I leaped out of bed like a man possessed and rushed to the back door. Missy was just lying there. We felt her body and found that her stomach had ballooned in size and was solid as a rock. We quickly picked her up and gently put her in the back of our Ford station wagon. I sat in the boot (the trunk) of the car beside her.

We had called ahead so the vet could prepare for our arrival. The journey felt like an eternity. I looked into Missy's beautiful brown eyes and knew that she knew something wasn't right. When we reached the vet, Missy was taken and assessed. The vet said that she had bloat, which happened when Missy's stomach filled with gas, food, or even fluid, making it expand in size. The stomach then put pressure on all her other organs, and if not treated, it could be fatal. Missy was taken in for surgery and there was nothing we could do but pray.

I was frightened; I loved Missy and didn't want to lose her. I was only ten years old and hadn't experienced the challenging pain that death brings.

My dad took my older brother and I across the road to get some breakfast. He sat us both down and didn't sugarcoat it. "Boys, I'm afraid that Missy might not make it."

Hearing those words crushed me.

Missy didn't deserve this; she had shown us nothing but unconditional love, affection, and warmth. I was privileged to be exposed to that kind of love from an early age.

Missy wasn't in surgery for very long. We were heading back toward the vet's office when my dad received a phone call. I started to get hopeful thinking that maybe our Missy was going to be okay.

We walked inside the vet's surgery (or office), and the look on my dad's face was one of utter disbelief. He clearly didn't know how to break the news to us that she was gone. Dad doesn't like showing that he is in pain or even experiencing raw emotions, especially tears. But to see Dad break down like that made me break down as well. Missy had suffered a massive heart attack during the operation, and they couldn't save her.

Being exposed to death at that age is traumatic; you don't really understand the full extent of what you've lost until much later. You don't feel right inside at all; you feel like your heart has been torn in two and nothing can put it back together again. It's hard to understand the toll of death unless you've been through it, especially when you lose someone so close to you.

After that day, all I did was cry. There was this empty hole inside my heart; something was missing from our family. I didn't understand why this even happened. I prayed so hard, and yet it felt like God didn't answer me. I became upset and angry at God—how could he allow so much pain into my life already? I had a lot of questions but didn't seem to be getting any answers, which made me more confused and frustrated.

Death is probably the most challenging experience anyone has to go through, especially as a young kid. Sadly, death is an unfortunate part of life, and although we might not fully understand why there is death, it is important to know that

God has a reason and a perfect plan for everything, even if our finite minds can't comprehend it. I may not have seen what God was doing behind the scenes, but he was preparing me for something far more challenging to come...

It started out as any other day for me. I woke up, got dressed for school, did my chores, and was out the door by 7:45 a.m. We headed off to school as we would do every other day during the week. Do you ever have those moments where you feel like something bad is going to happen? Well, I had one of those feelings that day.

The day went rather smoothly at school, then Mom took us to do the weekly grocery shopping. We were at the checkout loading the groceries and Mom's mobile phone rang. It was my dad telling Mom to bring us home; Grandy had collapsed and needed to go to the hospital immediately. Everything then went into slow motion.

Now this was all God's mercy, as my dad would have been at work that day, but he was home when Grandma called him to say that Grandy had collapsed in the shower. My dad immediately called an ambulance for Grandma. He then called my mom to tell her. Mom dropped us at home and then went straight to the hospital. Mom recounted that the Lord had her remain calm the entire drive to the hospital. And she knew that God was in complete control of the situation.

The doctor told Mom that Grandy had been placed in an induced coma and was on life support. He had a brain stem stroke, the worst possible stroke, and he shouldn't have survived it. The doctor said that he was paralyzed from the neck down. Everyone that knew my grandy knew that he was a tough son of a gun and a stubborn fighter that didn't know when to give up. (A trait that I adopted in my own life.)

God—in his mercy and grace—spared Grandy to hear the gospel again and to have one last opportunity to respond to

God. My mom started talking to him even though he was in a coma. A doctor even told her that she should stop, as it was a waste of time because he couldn't hear anything. My mom, however, told the doctor very firmly that he was listening to everything she was saying.

The next morning felt like a world away. The doctors told Mom that they were bringing my grandy out of his coma slowly to see how much damage had been done to his brain. He had some movement to his right side, but his left side was still paralyzed. When they allowed Mom into the intensive care unit (ICU), my grandy was awake, and tears began streaming down his face when he saw her. Mom could see fear in his eyes, and she knew he needed the Lord, and if the doctors were right, he wasn't going to survive this.

Mom was left alone with Grandy for a few minutes, and she asked him if he heard her speaking during the night. He nodded his head, as if to say yes. My mom then asked him if he trusted Christ as his savior, and he turned his head away, ignoring Mom. Even after suffering a life-threatening stroke, Grandy still refused to accept Christ as his savior.

Here is the thing about stubborn people. They only need to meet a persistent person, one that keeps chipping away, piece by piece, until there is a breakthrough. And my mom is a faithful prayer warrior and extremely persistent when she wants something. If there's one lesson that you can take away from this book out of all the rest, it's that persistent prayer works!

Our pastor at the time called Mom and offered to come to pray and visit Grandy. Pastor Gonderman soon came to the hospital, and he and Mom were given a small window of time in ICU alone with Grandy. This was where God began to work.

Pastor Gonderman asked Grandy some questions, and at first Grandy kept ignoring him. But the more our pastor spoke, and the more Mom prayed, Grandy began to soften.

After ten minutes, Pastor Gonderman prayed and then asked Grandy to nod to indicate yes if he trusted Christ. Grandy nodded, with tears streaming down his face. After Mom had spent many years, months, days, and hours praying for Grandy to trust Christ, we could all finally rest knowing that he was safe in the arms of God. If Grandy was to die at any moment, we knew that we would see him again one day.

We watched God defy all the doctors' predictions and textbook mentalities over the next couple of weeks. Grandy came off life support five days later (Mother's Day) and survived with his left side paralyzed, but he still couldn't eat food. Another miracle was that God didn't let Grandy to lose his voice, which was unheard of with a brain stem stroke.

After three months in the hospital, Grandy went into a nursing home and God used him to be a witness for Christ and restore relationships that were damaged. My mom had the privilege to disciple my grandy, and we spent many hours at the nursing home talking to him about God and reading God's word to him. Despite the physical disabilities, there was nothing wrong with Grandy's intelligent brain; he was still on the ball and alert.

This next part of the story was the most emotional for me to write. Our whole family had experienced enormous challenges during this time with Grandy being in the hospital and nursing home. The emotional toll that it takes on your body, mind, and spirit can be crushing. If you were to ask me if I had any regrets during this time, I would say that sadly I do.

When I see my grandy again, I'll rush into his arms crying and tell him how sorry I am for not valuing our time together more. I spent the majority of Grandy's last moments with us playing on my stupid Nintendo DS console. I completely zoned out, and all my grandy wanted to do was connect with his grandson like we used to.

Several months later, Grandy suffered another brain stem stroke. After Grandy fought for five days, the Lord gave him eternal peace at last in his new home: heaven.

To this day, losing my grandy was one of the worst challenges I've ever had to experience. We shared so many special moments together. Whenever I was sick, he and Grandma would give up their day to look after me. And every afternoon after school, I would call him to tell him about my day. He always listened, and if I had a bad day, he'd say, "Don't worry, you'll have a better one tomorrow."

Then there were just those random acts of kindness that you didn't expect. It made me love him even more, and it was a perfect example for me to always show random acts of kindness to others.

I really believe that my grandy showed me consistently what it takes to overcome and lead forward. To not give up when things get tough. Grandy was a good leader, in my eyes, at least.

I remember the times when I'd sit on his knee in church. He was an amazing cook; every birthday, he'd make a cake with his famous custard. Every Christmas, he'd cook a roast for us all to enjoy.

But more than that, he taught me to be wise with my money, the importance of hard work, and to never give up. He instilled in me a good character and told me to always value my integrity. He also taught me how to use a computer and how to persistently go after what you want. My grandy was an unstoppable force; when that man put his mind to something, very little could prevent him from achieving it. Grandy and I got on so well, and I'm told I take after him. I'm so proud of that fact.

One day, Grandy was trying to show me how to build something from wood. I wasn't gifted at building things with my hands—that was given to my two brothers. I'm a different creative type. However, during this time, all I wanted to do was sit on the couch, watch Cartoon Network, eat junk food, and drink pub squash (an epic lemon-flavored Australian beverage).

I said to Grandy, "I'm tired; can't we just finish this off another time?"

He looked intently at me and said, "Jarred, don't put off for tomorrow what can be done today. People that say they will do it tomorrow are only creating a bad habit of laziness. If you continue to procrastinate in life, you will never get anywhere good."

After that experience with Grandy, I can proudly say that I have never been good at procrastination. In fact, I can't even remember a time that I have procrastinated over something. Because if I ever get anywhere near procrastinating, my Grandy's wise words will come flooding back to my mind, stopping me in my tracks.

When I was in school, I used to get teased and called "crazy" for finishing all my assignments well in advance. During business college, I was criticized for wanting feedback on one of my assignments weeks before it was due. The teacher remarked, "This isn't like school; we don't have the time to give feedback."

Grandy was the opposite of lazy; in fact, he did a three-year managerial course in twelve months. He suffered a heart attack during it, but he still did it.

After we lost Missy, Grandy couldn't bear to see his grandkids upset all the time, so he bought us a new German Shepherd puppy that we affectionately named Joy.

For all the love and care Grandy showed us, he wasn't perfect by any stretch of the imagination. He had a temper and lost control on several occasions over stupid things that weren't worth fighting for. He was proud and stubborn, and the only one to ever break that stubbornness in the end was God and my mom's persistent prayers.

Part of what I do and who I am is to make my grandy proud of me. I know that he has been watching me from up in heaven, so when I see him again, I'll hug him tight and tell him all my stories. I can't wait for that day.

The Traumatic Daze

Have you ever been in your car driving toward a set destination, but you end up somewhere else? This has happened to me on several occasions. When I arrived at the wrong place, I was in a bit of a daze wondering how on earth I ended up where I didn't even plan on going. I believe that many of us are walking around in a daze—we know where we want to go, and yet we end up somewhere completely out of the blue, and it leaves us in a state of confusion.

For many years, I walked around in a daze not able to see the traumatic experience that happened when I was six years old. When the fog cleared, I saw that what I had thought I had been dreaming about actually did happen to me. And the reality of that news was like a knife to my heart.

For weeks leading up to having clarity, I began to get flashbacks and glimpses into my past. Even though I never saw them together, I had this visual image of my dad in a rage and about to hit this young teenage boy. I could see the fear expressed on that boy's face. However, my mind couldn't put it all together. I was too afraid to ask my mom and dad about the meanings behind these flashbacks. Instead, I continued to walk around with the same dazed mind that I had since I was six—unaware that my mind had buried this trauma as a way of protecting me.

It was Father's Day 2020, and I was sitting at the dinner table with my family enjoying the conversation and meal. I can't remember how we got stuck on this part of the conversation, but Dad brought up someone's name from our old church. Something in my brain sparked a hidden memory and I asked, "Who is that?" (I'm not going to mention names.)

Dad replied, "He was the one who touched you."

Now by this point, my brain was beginning to put two and two together. All those dazed memories that kept coming up from time to time, well, some of them were real, and there was a reason for why they kept coming up.

One day, I was sitting on this boy's lap on the couch in the living room while my mom and his mom were in the kitchen preparing afternoon tea.

As I was sitting on this boy's lap, he put his hand down my pants and began to fondle my genitals for a solid fifteen seconds. He then took his hand out and stared sharply at me and said, "If you tell anyone, I'll hurt you."

I just laughed it off because I was too young to understand what had just happened.

The next day, Mom was vacuuming the house when I blurted out that this boy had touched my private parts. I don't really remember what happened next, apart from my dad's face when he found out.

I was sexually abused as a six-year-old boy by a fifteen-year-old boy who should have known better. It wasn't the act itself that was the challenge—the challenge was the trauma I experienced because of the act. Because of the trauma, my brain created the daze as a way of protecting how I interacted with people from then on. It was a defense mechanism.

During my first semester of university, I wrote a thesis on trauma and how it impacts the brain. Did you know that the leading cause of high anxiety, stress, depression, and even death in young adults is due to some form of trauma? When a young person experiences a traumatic event either in the family, in their personal health, or even witnessing a death, it can cause post-traumatic stress disorder (PTSD) and feelings of fear, sadness, guilt, and sometimes pain, This leads to a young person feeling anxious, depressed, stressed, and in some cases, they can go through the horrific act of suicide.

PTSD affects 5–10 percent of the general population. That is millions of people, including children, who if left untreated will have to deal with high levels of stress, anxiety, and depression.

I went on to further explain that there needed to be more research conducted into trauma to figure out better strategies around how we could help people dealing with past or present traumas.

I was once fortunate to have a powerful and deep conversation with a ninety-four-year-old Auschwitz survivor. She endured a horrific traumatic experience—yet she said to me, "The reality is, that when you were touched, your childhood ended."

Sadly, she was right. The moment that the experience happened, it was like my mind went into defense mode, clouding over the thoughts of it even happening. At such a young age, you don't really comprehend or understand these kinds of experiences, and you therefore have no way to navigate how it affects you.

At the age of fourteen, I was dealing with depression and anxiety. And at seventeen years of age, I experienced a severe panic attack and high amounts of stress that often made me sick.

During my childhood, I spent a lot of time in either the doctor's office or in the hospital with some unexplained illness. I believe that part of the reason (aside from some physical illnesses) was due to experiencing sexual trauma. Research has shown me that trauma will stay with you for the rest of your life—it won't ever go away.

And the most challenging part about trauma isn't actually going through it—it's dealing with the aftermath of it. I never opened up to anyone about what happened because I was afraid of what people would think of me. Another boy sexually assaulted me, and I was ashamed of it. I kept the pain inside, and I allowed the daze to continue. I even saw psychologists, but I never spoke about how I was feeling inside. Perhaps if I had shared my thoughts and feelings, it might have helped more. I'll never know.

If you have gone through trauma of any kind, I understand how hard it can be to move forward from it. Just because dealing with the aftereffects of trauma can be challenging doesn't mean you can't put strategies in place to help you manage it.

I want you to understand something. Everyone at some point in their life has experienced trauma of some kind. You aren't alone, and the first management strategy that I can give you is simple, but also hard to implement.

Go and speak with someone you trust. I should have talked to someone sooner about the daze I was living in, but I chose to keep my feelings locked away, hidden from even the ones that I loved most. I understand that it takes a brave amount of courage to be vulnerable with someone, but as you start to express your feelings more, you begin to heal. There is comfort and safety in the presence of a trusted friend.

You can and will get through this. Don't let the challenges break you; instead, let them serve you as building blocks for your progress forward and allow them to give you the wind to soar upon.

CHAPTER 4

The Blinding Ego

Sometimes, All You Need Is a Near-Death Experience to Put Your Life Back into Perspective

There have been four occasions when I almost died. The first was when I was two years old, which I'll share in a later chapter. But since then, there have been two other occasions when God has almost taken me home. One when I selfishly decided that I wanted to go home early, which I'll talk about in a later chapter as well. However, for some reason, God chose to save me and keep me here; God definitely has something big planned for my life, and I can't wait to experience what that is.

I was fourteen, young, fit, and somewhat healthy even after my kidney ordeal. I exercised mostly every day, and I enjoyed basketball more than any other sport I was playing at the time.

It began on Monday, September 13, 2010, when I woke up feeling aches and pains in my body. I had a sore throat, headache, stomachache, and nausea. And these symptoms lasted until Wednesday evening, but by then my body aches and sore throat had gone away. I went off to bed, and later that night I awoke with nausea and severe stabbing pains in the middle of my stomach.

I once again tried to be the big, brave tough guy and decided not to tell Mom of my symptoms until the next morning. The stabbing pains and nausea continued, but I still went to school. Mom worked at the school as the receptionist (I know, blessed—right?).

And later that same morning after half an hour of being in the sick bay (the nurse's office), I was in so much pain that I wanted to vomit. Mom took me to the office bathroom where she stayed with me. The school principal (fun fact: she had known me since I was a baby) told us she would call an ambulance.

I was sitting in the school reception area waiting for the ambulance to arrive when I had this uncontrollable urge to vomit, and I couldn't stop vomiting from then on. All I was bringing up was bile. The ambulance finally arrived, and they rushed me to hospital. Seeing as the Westmead Children's Hospital was unavailable at the time, the ambulance took me to another hospital that was close by.

When I arrived at the hospital, I was taken care of by a wonderful nurse who hooked me up to a bag of fluids, pain relief, and she also organized blood tests.

Once Mom arrived, she told the emergency nurse that she was concerned that it could be my appendix. (Mom had had the same symptoms back in 2006, but her story is crazier than mine! She almost died too.)

I didn't present with all the typical appendicitis symptoms, which was why the nurse thought it might be just a bad tummy bug. I had had a severe stomach bug years prior, and trust me, this pain was far worse. Mum was starting to get a bit anxious at this stage because I hadn't even been seen to by a doctor yet and I was getting worse.

When the emergency doctor finally examined me, she wasn't sure what was wrong and said that she would call for a surgical consult. By this stage, I was referring to my pain level as twenty out of ten, and I was continuing to bring up green bile. The pain relief wasn't helping at all, and after hours of waiting and asking the nurse and doctor when I would be seen to by a surgeon, I heard from the nurse that she was unable to give me a time.

That afternoon, a trainee surgeon came to examine me. With arms crossed, he said, "What's up with you?"

I tried to explain what I was feeling, and of course Mom had to help fill in some of the gaps. The trainee told me to get out of bed and jump on my right leg, which was extremely difficult to do, but I did it anyway. I got back onto the bed and then the doctor asked me, "What's your pain level like?"

I told him that it was well over ten.

He laughed at me and said, "Well, you don't look like you're in too much pain to me, mate."

I couldn't (and still can't) believe a doctor would be this arrogant. But sadly, some doctors think they know everything.

Mom asked the trainee surgeon what was going to happen to me.

He replied, "Well, he doesn't have typical appendicitis at this stage. The pain isn't typical, he has no temp, and while his blood tests are indicating an infection, that could be just a tummy bug. We'll monitor him, keep up his fluids and pain relief, and I'll do a laparoscopy in the morning." He also said, "It could be that his stomach lymph nodes on the right side are inflamed, which is common."

Mom then asked if anything was going to be done today.

The trainee then replied, "I have another surgery, and he'll be fine until the morning."

That's when Mom expressed her concerns about my appendix, but he didn't appear to be too worried about that.

My mom then asked, "What happens if Jarred deteriorates during the night? Will he have surgery here?"

The trainee just looked at Mom, smiled, and said rather rudely, "*No!* I'll do him first thing in the morning."

"So, what happens if his appendix bursts during the night?" Mom asked.

The trainee surgeon proudly replied, "It won't burst." (A statement he'd later regret uttering.)

Mom then told him that she had been misdiagnosed when she had appendicitis, and because of this, her appendix had burst.

But he just smiled and said, "Well, I won't put him on antibiotics, as this will mask the symptoms. We'll admit him to a ward and wait and see how he goes. If he gets worse during the night, we'll put him on antibiotics, which will settle him down."

And with that, the trainee surgeon left.

My mom then shared her concerns again with the emergency doctor who had first assessed me. She said that she understood Mom's concerns, but she tried to assure us all that I would be taken care of. At this stage, Mom asked for a second opinion, and the doctor said it wasn't possible.

My dad arrived and he stayed to look after me while Mom went home to check on my two brothers. Mom also called the Westmead Children's Hospital to see if she could request a transfer. She spoke with a nurse who told Mom to go back and ask if I was going to go into surgery if my health deteriorated. If they said no, then they would put in a request to have me transferred to the Westmead Children's Hospital. Suddenly, the hospital became available if needed.

When Mom arrived back at the hospital, she spoke with the nurse who had been taking care of me the whole time and the triage doctor. The nurse could clearly see that I was deteriorating, and she seemed concerned. To me, there was more concern than actual action. Mom asked them both if the hospital did emergency surgery during the night, and if not then she wanted me transferred to the Westmead Children's Hospital, or my parents were taking me there themselves.

The nurse just looked down at the floor, but she was giving the impression that Mom was just overreacting.

That's the moment when I yelled out, "Will you just get this bloody thing out. I'm in pain!"

That seemed to do the trick, because the nurse decided to go over the trainee surgeon's head and bring in the head surgeon.

The head surgeon arrived with the trainee surgeon who had assessed me before. He then ordered a medical drug to be given to me called Soma (also known as carisoprodol), but the Soma drug didn't work.

When Mom asked whether it could be an appendicitis, the head surgeon replied, "I'm not sure, as Jarred's pain is now under the bottom of his right rib cage." He even made the judgement call that it could be a tumor. He ordered a chest x-ray. This was to check whether my lungs were okay for surgery.

Dad then tried to share the journey he had with Mom when she had complications with her appendix, and that's when the trainee surgeon waved his hand and said, "Ah, that's enough of that; I don't want to hear it."

Sheer frustration and anger were clearly depicted on Dad's face. He even had to wait outside; it was obvious that he was close to expressing these emotions toward the trainee surgeon. And even though the circumstances were worrying, and I was still in so much pain, I couldn't help but smile while imagining Dad carrying out what I knew he wanted to do.

As the head surgeon and trainee were walking out, the trainee said, "If you choose to go public, I'll be doing the surgery, but if you choose to go private, the head surgeon will be doing the surgery."

Well, for obvious reasons, we went private.

I was given more pain relief and another Soma to help relieve some of the pain, which did help stop my constant vomiting. I was then admitted and taken to a ward at around 7:30 p.m., and at 9:15 p.m., we went into theatre (what some of you may know as the operating room).

This was when I began to get a temperature. And when you have a temperature, it's usually a sign that your appendix has burst. And mine had!

To make matters worse, when I was in surgery, I woke up right when my appendix was being taken out!

I then heard the surgeon say to the nurse beside him, "We'll just tell his mom that it burst in my hands."

I even saw the surgeon place my appendix, which was filled with fluid and puss, into a small clear tube. That's the moment I fell back to sleep.

At 11:45 p.m., the head surgeon came out, and Mom said to him, "Well, was it his appendix?"

The head surgeon wouldn't look at my mum and kept looking at his feet. He then replied, "Yes, it was."

My mom asked, "Had it burst?"

The head surgeon replied, "Yes."

(But he didn't tell her when it had burst.)

Mom then asked whether there was an infection in my abdomen, and while still looking at his feet, the head surgeon replied, "Yes."

My mom said, "If he died, you'd have had to live with that. Both you and the trainee surgeon would have had to. Next time, listen to your patients."

I was thinking, *damn, way to go, Mom.*

The next morning, the trainee surgeon came to examine me. (The head surgeon didn't have the integrity to do it himself. His ego was far too inflated for that.) He told me that I could go home if I was feeling up to it. When Mom asked him if I'd need to take any antibiotics while I was back home, he said it wouldn't be necessary.

So, I decided to stay until Saturday to get at least forty-eight hours of antibiotics.

And this was a wise decision…

During my recovery at home, Mom called the head surgeon to ask what could be done about my wounds. He told her to leave it alone and to see him in three weeks' time if it got worse. If the wound became sore, then we'd know it was worse.

Mom decided to take me to the GP, and upon examining the wound, he found that it was infected. I was given more antibiotics and had the wound redressed for another two weeks until the infection cleared. If I didn't stay in hospital for those two extra days on antibiotics, the wound would have become far worse.

I wasn't your average textbook case. And unfortunately, the terrible old-fashioned bedside manner and lack of humility from both the trainee and head surgeon almost cost me my life.

Remove the Ego

Here is what I learned from my second near-death experience: pride will always come before a fall. Just because you have a degree from a university doesn't always mean you know everything. Good medical staff will always listen to their patients, and experience is and always will be the best teacher. Never allow pride to direct your decisions, especially if you have someone's life on the line. Because after all, a person's life is priceless!

Ego is a big issue for a lot of people today, including myself. An ego won't take you anywhere good mentally, spiritually, or emotionally. Always remember that without your work, you are nothing but blood, bones, and muscle. We are all human; no one is better than another, so try and show humility.

It's scary to think that because of two people's ego, I could have died. When you allow ego into your heart and mind, it takes over. Sometimes, ego just creeps its ugly head out of the cracks you've left unguarded and *bam*—the hurt begins. Ego wants control, as it thrives off it—so don't keep feeding it. Don't be so blind, like those surgeons were, to think you know best.

Practice being honest and open with yourself, and make sure you forgive yourself when you do slip and let ego take over. It honestly doesn't take much for someone's ego to cause a lot of destruction.

I truly believe that children have the purest of hearts and often don't have egos. When I was growing up, I didn't fear anything, and if you asked me what an ego was back then, I'd have probably replied with, "Huh?" It's because as we grow and mature, and we have more experiences, we begin to develop more awareness to ideas, emotions, and feelings. The naivety of a child is suddenly replaced with learned behaviors like ego-centric beliefs.

The ego is a trickster at times, and it's quite clever at deceiving even the most cunning of minds. Just think how many lives could have been spared during wars or wars prevented from even happening if people in positions of power controlled their egos.

How can we remove ego from our lives? Is that even possible?

Well, yes, it's definitely possible for a period of time.

The first step to removing an ego is identifying that it exists in your life. And then guess what? You've just completed the most difficult part of reworking an ego-driven mind.

It's interesting when someone tells you that you've got a giant ego, as immediately the ego says to your mind and subconscious, *You don't have an ego problem.* If you listen to that voice, it's a perfect indication that you *do* have an ego problem.

Once you have identified that ego exists in your life, it's time to begin healing and removing it from your life. And there is no reason to beat yourself up over having an ego. This is an unhealthy but sadly normal habit of many people. What often happens is that the ego doesn't want to be removed, so it fights back, and we let it. When the ego fights, it creates damage to your emotional, spiritual, mental, and physical state of being. Remember that the weak will never forgive themselves—that's only for the strong.

What are you going to be: strong or weak?

Practice surrendering daily. When we fight back, ego wins, but when we surrender to the fact that we are being proud, ego loses. It actually takes more strength to surrender than to fight back. Because that's what the ego wants. And you aren't surrendering to your ego; you're surrendering to the fact it needs to be removed and to the healing steps that come as a result of that surrender. Removing your ego is a daily practice.

Practice moments of self-love and self-care.

Spend time alone at a local café. A friend once told me to take myself on a date. There's no shame in wanting to be alone occasionally. We need to learn to enjoy silent moments.

The ego loves busy environments and thrives in them.

Did you know that the eagle is a selfless bird? The eagle has one important practice that it does on a consistent basis. An eagle practices selfless acts of love for either their children or their mate. The eagle's babies know that their mother will bring them food as a way of taking care of them and showing unconditional, selfless love. It would be easy for the mother eagle to just keep all the food to herself, or not even go hunting for food. Yet she does it willingly. She gives a majority of the food to her kids first, then if there is any left at the end, that's when she eats too, with her mate.

I believe that we should all learn from this important practice. When ego is present, be like the eagle—be selfless, not selfish.

Remember to breathe and tell yourself it's going to be okay. Because it will be, my friends. You have a choice to let your ego take control over your life or rise above it every day—like an eagle.

Just fourteen days after my appendix burst, we went on a family holiday to Queensland that we had booked a couple of months prior to my "incident." The recovery process wasn't going to stop me from going on my holiday; I deserved some time out.

The head surgeon had said that I was still able to go, but to stay out of the sun, not to go swimming, to keep hydrated, and to try to relax. However, do you think that I did any of those things? Of course not! I was always up early going fishing with my dad, running along the beach, kayaking—having very minimal rest, if any at all. That's my idea of a holiday.

The last day before we had to leave Queensland and drive all the way back to New South Wales, my older brother Nathan and I decided to go kayaking one last time. We were out in the hot sun; it felt like thirty-five degrees Celsius (ninety-five degrees Fahrenheit) that day. I had no sunscreen, no water, and I was sitting at the back of the kayak doing most of the steering.

When we arrived back to shore, I was burned to a crisp and felt tired. Despite that, I didn't sleep at all that night, and my head was pounding. The following morning, I awoke with my head still pounding, but with the added benefit of it spinning. My body was also aching, but then again, I just put it down to all the high-intensity paddling I did the day before. So, I once again decided to put the pain aside and drank some apple juice and proceeded to pack the car bound for home.

We were about one hour into the trip home when I told Mom that I wasn't feeling well at all. She gave me a vomit bag just in case, and well, it wasn't long after that that I began throwing up. The motion of the car certainly didn't help either. The vomiting kept going; we even had to stop a few times so I could vomit on the side of the road because we ran out of vomit bags.

It was clear to Mom that something was wrong with me. So, we made a "quick" pit stop, and guess where? That's right, the hospital! We were seen to immediately, which was a huge blessing. I was placed on fluids for about four hours to get my body hydrated again. It turned out that I suffered severe heat exhaustion. This was where our family phrase "Oh, what is another hospital trip for Jay?" was born. So far, I had been to the hospital more times than I cared to count. I have only mentioned a few of them in this book so far, but there were many other times that I was taken to hospital for numerous illnesses.

A lot can happen when you are just fourteen years old. This is an age where you're trying to figure out life, go through puberty, and form ideas, values, opinions, and character traits. I understand that you learn throughout life, but the ages of fourteen to eighteen are a crucial time for any young person's development. I believe that I was blessed to go through so much already before I turned fifteen. It woke me up to some important life lessons that many people are still trying to learn today.

You just don't know when your time on Earth will end. Having to go through all this pain early on in my life gave me more appreciation for what I currently have in my life. Never take anything in life for granted. And don't let your ego place you in a state of being ungrateful. I've been ungrateful many times before, so you aren't alone if you have experienced this.

You only have one precious life, which is a gift. You were created and formed with a unique and special purpose. It doesn't matter how you began your life or where you are right now on your journey. What matters is your attitude while on each path that you end up on.

Don't forget that you have one life, just one, that's it. You don't get any do-overs. This isn't a simulation or a game, this life is real; it should be cherished. So start making the most of this life and don't allow pride and ego to blind you along the way.

Have eagle vision and keep on soaring.

CHAPTER 5

Suffering in "Perfect" Silence

Silence When You Are Suffering Is Not Golden

Depression is very real, and it affects the lives of many people. Sadly, depressed people can often remain quiet about it, like I did for a long time. After all, who likes hearing about the fact someone is depressed? No one likes being around a person who is constantly miserable all the time. For those people who are depressed, it is rather lonely.

I read a very alarming statistic not long ago that one in every three men in Australia alone will commit suicide, and four men commit suicide every day.

Just think about that for a moment. Four people have passed on into eternity because of depression. (This was before the pandemic, but because of the pandemic that number has since increased, which is alarming and should concern you.)

Because they thought no one loved them.

Because they believed no one cared.

Because they think they are alone.

I'm not saying that depression is the main cause of why people want to commit suicide; however, according to evidence found in so many cases of suicidal deaths, depression was largely a contributing factor.

Identifying Depression

Depression often goes under the radar, as some people are good at hiding it. Depression is not just feeling sad about yourself. Imagine for a moment that you no longer enjoy all the things you used to enjoy. You get a feeling of numbness toward life, and nothing brings you joy, satisfaction, or happiness. Depression can come from a traumatic experience, loss of a loved one, emotional, physical, sexual, or even verbal abuse. The truth is, there are so many reasons as to why we can become depressed.

We all have those days where we feel disconnected from life and ourselves. We all have those days when we feel down; trust me, I've been there more times than I care to count. But just because you're having a bad day doesn't mean you are depressed.

Depression comes from consistently hurting on the inside.

The reason why so many people become depressed in the first place is because they choose to allow those negative thoughts to overtake the mind, body, and spirit. And I know that there are other factors that do contribute, such as chemical imbalances in the brain and body. Because of these reasons, depression then takes its place in our inner psyche—it *controls* what we believe, think, and do.

I've never admitted this to anyone before, but I eventually got to the point where I had allowed my thoughts (not beliefs, as there is a difference) to form beliefs that caused me to want to end it all. I didn't tell anyone that I was suicidal—I even thought of how I was going to end it all. I was just fed up with all the pain and suffering I had endured over the years. I felt worthless and that no one would ever love me. I felt alone.

The reason why so many people commit suicide is because they have lost all hope and no longer want to live with the pain. They think the pain will end when their life ends, but it doesn't. What about the people who are left behind with the knowledge that you ended your life? That's why suicide is ultimately a selfish act. You may be out of pain, but you've left more pain for your friends and family.

As a man, I know the kind of struggles we go through with our mental health. Society and culture conditioned us to believe that we are meant to look, act, and speak a certain way. I became very good at suffering in silence for many years because I was conditioned to believe that showing any emotion, failing at something, not looking as if I was in control under pressure meant that I wasn't strong. I thought it meant that I wasn't a man. Because, after all, a man is meant to hold it all together, right? But these are just ridiculous, false beliefs that I had been taught and kept close to my heart for years!

Here is what I have learned over my lifetime about what it means to be a real man.

> A real man will choose to *forgive* rather than not forgive and end up harboring bitterness and resentment in his heart.

> A real man will seek out the truth and isn't afraid of rejection from asking questions.

> A real man in the face of adversity will hold true to what he believes in.

A real man seeks wise counsel and chooses his friends carefully, for he understands that he will become who he hangs around.

A real man is faithful and is committed to all areas of his life, and not just some.

A real man knows when to walk away from a fight and when to engage in one.

A real man admits when he has done wrong and will openly apologize to those he has wronged.

A real man treats everyone with respect and dignity, and a real man values his integrity above all else.

A real man is kind, generous, and selfless.

A real man opens the door for a lady, young or old—it doesn't matter—and he will also give up his seat for a lady.

A real man isn't afraid to be vulnerable. He's courageous in his actions. He loves God with all his heart, mind, body, and soul.

A real man leads his life from what he believes to be true. He doesn't follow the crowds, as the crowds are easily followed. He leads with love so that others may look to his example and do the same.

Sadly, society has produced more boys than men. It makes boys feel like becoming a man is too difficult, and so those boys feel helpless. They would much rather follow the crowds than stand up and search out real meaning and truth. Instead, we have a society that spoon-feeds this generation lies. It's no wonder so many males in our world today struggle with mental health problems.

I'm putting my hand up in this scenario and saying that this was me for many years. When it came to my mental health, I believed all the lies: I was worthless, no good, and would never amount to anything. Social and mainstream media thrive on these lies too. It's a tool now for people to use and abuse emotions, and sadly, many fall into these traps of unbelief in the self.

When I left school, I began working for several after-school care companies. I would have children as young as six come and tell me things no six-year-old should ever know about. It's alarming to think that these young minds are being polluted and indoctrinated with such vile ideas. Sadly, childhood is often where it all begins for many. And it's the exact place where it needs to end, too. Remember: silence is not golden.

I understand what it's like to not want to speak up to someone. It did more harm to me than good. Please don't be afraid to speak up. It could save your life or someone else's. I want to encourage anyone suffering out there that if you are struggling, you also have the power to change all of that. Remember that there is a way out.

Allow me to show you, and I honestly hope and pray that my story will inspire that change and transformation for you.

The First Time I Suffered in Silence

I met this beautiful young girl who had just started at my high school. I was eighth grade and she was about to begin seventh grade. Now, I was not popular at all in school—quite the opposite. She, on the other hand, was popular because of her charm and looks. Keep in mind, it was a small school, so the moment someone new arrived, we all experienced that wave of excitement, especially if the new person was a young, good-looking girl.

When she started to take notice of little old me, I was instantly struck by the fact that a stunning girl was even talking to me. I didn't have a great deal of self-esteem or confidence back then. But just like a mouse is attracted to the smell of the cheese on a trap, not knowing it's going to be a trap to kill them, I was attracted to her. We began Skyping every afternoon after school. We couldn't get enough of each other, and everything seemed normal until that quickly changed.

This was just the beginning of a very long, tormenting period of manipulative and emotional abuse.

It wasn't long after we had begun Skyping that she introduced me to a new world I never thought existed—the world of mental health, which included depression, anxiety, self-harm, emotional and physical abuse, and endless amounts of stress and worry.

One day, I was on a call with her, and she pulled out a razor blade. I asked her what the blade was for. She remarked that it was for cutting her wrists. I had to watch her cut open her wrists, blood going everywhere, and I couldn't do anything about it. If I said something, she would hang up the call, and I'd freak out thinking she was going to kill herself, and I would be the one to blame, as there were times when she told me that was what she was going to do.

I was terrified; I'd never seen or heard of this type of manipulation or behavior before. I tried—with my limited knowledge and understanding of what mental health was—to help this girl. I thought that I could become her hero, her savior, and her knight in shining armor because this was what I believed I was supposed to do, thanks to society's teachings.

Let me tell you an important truth: you can't be the hero, and you certainly can't remove any of the demons that another person is suffering with. The only way someone is going to change is when they *decide* to change. I understand that men generally want to fix things, but there are things that you can't fix. All you can do is encourage and be there as much as humanly possible for someone who is suffering while also taking care of your own mental health. The more you force someone to get out of their state of mental illness, the more they will dive further in.

This entire situation was something I needed to get away from, and fast. But do you think that's what I did? No, definitely not! Instead, I went all in, head over heels. As a result, all it did was plunge me into a depressed state of mind. I distanced myself from my friends at school. I told my mom I hated life and that I wanted to just get away from it all. And when she'd ask me what was wrong, I'd make up stories to mask what was really happening. My parents had no idea a girl from school was causing their son to be depressed.

As a result of how I was behaving, my friends at school clearly didn't know how to act around me. It was like they were walking on eggshells all the time. I didn't tell them what was really going on out of fear that I'd lose this girl. She used to tell me that no one would ever love me again if I left her.

She was also really close with her best guy friend, who happened to be her ex-boyfriend. There were a few occasions where she would tell me we were over, then go to her ex-boyfriend, start "dating" him for two days, then come back to me. That emotional turmoil happened quite often. Keep in mind that I was only fourteen, and I had never experienced anything like this before, so I didn't really know any better. Like I said previously, fourteen is a crucial age of forming your identity and ideas about life. My start threw me into the negative world of mental health issues.

My parents became worried about me. I even mentioned that I had suicidal thoughts, which clearly frightened Mom. Even though I wasn't going to go through with suicide at that time, my parents didn't take any chances. In truth, I was just venting my frustrations out in all the wrong ways and to all the wrong people, who didn't deserve to be treated like that.

Finally, after many heated arguments with Mom, I agreed to see a psychologist. Her name was Lyn. She was a sweet and kindhearted lady with a warm and gentle personality. Her presence lit up a room.

However, I didn't have the right attitude going into our first meeting. And she could obviously see right through me. We both sat down, and her first question startled me a bit. "So, why do you think you need to be here?"

I looked at her in silence for a while. She was patient and just smiled while waiting for me to respond. I asked her if my mom would know anything about what we discussed. She assured me that nothing would leave the room. That's when I began to open up about everything that was happening. One thing about Lyn was that she made me feel comfortable with expressing my feelings. She was exceptional at empathizing with me and comforting me when she could see there was pain inside.

The situation that I had put myself in had taken its toll on all aspects of my life. I wasn't sleeping or eating, which meant that I had no energy at all, and I started losing weight. This then affected my hormones and in turn impacted my mood. I was angry and frustrated all the time and often lashed out at those closest to me. I felt like I had more stress than a solider in combat.

I saw Lyn for weeks, and each time we spoke, she would give me strategies to help with what was going on. She never forced me to break up with the girl, nor did she have a judgmental tone about any of it. I felt safe with Lyn. I knew that I needed to change, but I was just too afraid, so the abuse and depression kept on for months even after I turned fifteen.

The First Change

I was in the living room of my grandparents' house (we were living there looking after the house as my grandma was in the nursing home) one day, and at this point, I can't remember how long I had been depressed for. But quite a while.

My "girlfriend" called me on Skype, and we began a casual conversation. She then brought her best girlfriend on the call. We engaged in conversation, but it wasn't long before my girlfriend got into *a mood*. And the reason for this mood was that she wanted to see my penis and show it to her best girlfriend too. But I had repeatedly said no.

I didn't say anything in response to the mood at first, and each time I said no, she would hang up on me. I tried calling her back several times, but to no avail. She then finally called me, and I said that I would show her mine if she showed me hers. She agreed, and well...I showed her, but then she and her girlfriend giggled and hung up on me, just like that. And so, I finally said to myself that enough was enough. I had given this girl so much, and she had given me nothing but grief and pain. I even went as far as showing her my private parts and that still wasn't enough. I closed my laptop and went off to bed feeling utterly ashamed.

My phone, however, wouldn't stop buzzing during the night, but for the first time I found myself ignoring it. In truth, I was just done with it all. Lyn's advice, and even my parents' advice, came flooding into my mind.

That was when I made a choice. The choice to end my depression. To step out of the darkness and into the light.

And finally, when I did that, I felt like I had control over the situation and my emotions at the same time. Instead of thinking that I was worthless and not good enough for anyone, I flipped my thought process to: *I know I'm worth more than what she thinks I am.* I wasn't going to conform to her will anymore. I took away the control she had over me.

I realized in that moment as I was lying in bed that all I was to her was nothing but a piece of meat available at her beck and call. I understood that night that for me to change, I needed to change my current mindset, and that it was ultimately my choice to change. It was like an old light bulb had burst and a new one had been put in its place.

There is a saying that I came up with: "If you tell yourself you can't, then you won't. If you tell yourself you can, then you will."

I wish I had known my own saying back when I was struggling with depression. The power of knowing that you can do something is extremely valuable, especially if you're struggling through mental health problems.

The next morning, I finally felt free. It was a feeling I hadn't experienced in a long—and I mean a long, long—time. The feelings of shame and guilt were no more. This was new because my mentality on life was new. I blurted out to Mom on our way to school that I was no longer depressed, and I clearly almost gave Mom a heart attack from shock. She asked me all these questions to see if I wasn't just fabricating another lie. And this time, it was the truth: I really wasn't depressed anymore.

I went back to see Lyn a few days later and told her the good news. I told her everything that happened. She was proud that I was able to control the situation and that I was no longer numb to life.

There was so much more to that part of my life, which I won't go into. But what I will say is that you have the power to change your current state of mind. If your depression is chemically induced, then go and seek help too. Don't delay! I finally understood that I did have a choice. All of us have a choice.

So, what choice will you make?

The Ugly Lies People Believe

Have you ever lied to someone that you love? Sadly, I know I have on many occasions. To tell you the truth, it feels good to lie. But trust me, the moment you get caught, that good feeling no longer exists.

Let me share another powerful truth for you. It's so easy for us to lie—it's like we are programmed to do it. Have you ever been in a situation where you have two options: you could either tell the truth and risk the consequences; or you could lie and avoid the consequences a bit longer and make them far worse than what they have to be? When we lie, we not only damage our own trust, but the trust of others.

I believe that many people become masters at lying to themselves. Some continue to walk through life thinking it's okay to lie and that they will get away with it. Trust me, one day those lies will come back to bite you on the butt! They have for me on many occasions.

That old saying "Fake it until you make it" is just teaching people not to be authentic—to basically live a lie until you do it so much that you start to believe that lie. Why do you think there are so many people struggling with purpose, self-worth, belief, and value? It's because they don't know how to be authentically true to themselves.

The worst offenders are those suffering through depression. Men are especially great at this. We hide behind walls and facades built on lies we choose to believe. We would rather retreat from our emotions than face them and hear the truth.

Here are just twenty-one ugly lies people believe.

(I purposely focused on men, as I am one.)

1. I'm not worth anything.
2. I won't ever be good enough.
3. I'll never find or be loved.
4. I'm ugly.
5. I've failed too many times to be given another chance.
6. I wouldn't bet on me.
7. Nobody likes me.
8. Being too emotional is only for girls.
9. To be a man, I need a six-pack.
10. Women only want men with big penises.
11. No one will accept a fatty.
12. There is no such thing as a "real man."
13. I don't need help from anyone.
14. I need to be the hero all the time.
15. Women need me, but I don't need them.
16. What's the point of anything?
17. Money will always make me happy and fulfilled.
18. I need to sleep with as many women as possible to be a man.
19. I don't believe in mental illness.
20. I am immune to stress.
21. I don't have any confidence.

People will tell themselves all of these lies at some point in their life. Men have become so great at believing these lies, and it's no wonder, given that the rate of suicide among men is three times higher than that for women. I know there are so many more lies men tell themselves. I want to point out that each of these lies are just lies we choose to believe. They aren't real! Please don't think that they are.

I read another alarming statistic that the most common age range among men who commit suicide is between the ages of fourteen and twenty-four years old. As men, we are often conditioned to believe these lies—we must look, dress, act, or speak a certain way to be a man. No woman is going to want to be with you if you can't provide financially, if you don't have a rocking hot body, or if you can't dress the part. I felt the exact same pressure growing up.

Being a real man today is what I mentioned above, it's knowing who you are. You don't always need to know where you're going, even though that's what parents, friends, or even social media tell you that you *should* know.

As you grow from a teenager to a young adult (fourteen to twenty-four), you are still trying to find your place in society. You are still trying to form ideas and values. Many young men fall into the trap of believing these lies, and often they don't know any better. It's just how they have been taught.

A great deal of men suffer from mental health issues due to lies they choose to believe. I do understand there are biological and chemical imbalances that occur for some men, like I have mentioned before. But from my conversations with leading health experts on my podcast, most of the time, the lies men choose to believe based around negative traumatic experiences are often the culprits.

I believed all of these lies when I was just fourteen! It has taken me many years to work through them all. Not believing these lies won't just happen overnight—trust me, I wish it did. Even when I chose to leave that toxic relationship, it didn't mean that I still didn't have inner demons to battle. To be completely honest with you, I have accepted those negative lies from time to time, and if I'm not careful, they will come up again to try and cause me pain. I've just become stronger at subduing them.

I discovered a very powerful method to help with dealing with lies, depression, anxiety, stress, negative beliefs, and not knowing your own self-worth. This method can also be applied to what I'm going to touch on in my next chapter about addictions. This method has helped me many times, and to my knowledge, it's helped several people get back control over their minds.

The CAP Method

I've never really been great at acronyms, yet here I am creating one. The irony, right! The CAP method, as I call it, helped me when I was battling mental health and addictions in 2019. I wish I had used this method when I was fifteen.

I like to say, "Let's put a CAP on all your problems and negative thoughts and seal it tight so it's extremely hard to open." I wish it were possible to get rid of all our problems, lies, and negative beliefs, but sadly, we can't. However, the good news is that we can learn how to better manage them.

This method is more of a helpful guide that you can use to work through your problems daily. I guarantee that if you use this method on a persistently consistent basis, you'll notice some drastic changes in your mindset and therefore your quality of life.

How do I know this?

Because I live by this method every single day, and it's helped me immensely. The best part about this method is that it's simple yet effective, so anyone can apply it to their life right now. But once again, it's your choice to do it or not.

I have a few sayings that helped form the CAP method.

One: "Don't make the choice to say you can't; instead, say that you can."

Two: "Each day, one must learn to accept if he or she is ever going to find peace."

Three: "Be persistent to remain consistent at the things you want."

C = Choice

Whether you believe this or not, or whether you are religious or not—God has given us an incredible gift called "free will." The ability for us to make decisions in our lives is always going to be due to consequences of our *choices*, whether good or bad. God gave this same gift to the angels in heaven.

One called Lucifer made the choice to believe a lie that he was better than God. He made the choice to allow his ego—which then turned into pride—control his heart. The moment he did that, he was cast out of heaven with countless others that followed his bad leadership.

As I mentioned earlier, removing one's ego is difficult but not impossible. It's because of sin that it's a constant struggle to remove one's ego. For some reason, men struggle with this more than women do—it's ingrained within us.

To discuss choice further, I will refer again to a conversation I had with New South Wales former police commissioner Andrew Scipione. I asked him how he was able to be so calm in the face of uncertainty, especially after witnessing a tragic event. His response changed my life.

"There are tough days, Jarred, really tough days. But you must make a choice. Pain is inevitable when you're a cop; you'll go home thinking about all the terrible things that have happened during the day, like a baby that has died in a cot, or a parent that's been stabbed by a person under the influence of drugs. But how you allow the misery to affect you—that's optional. The only person that is going to allow the pain to affect you is you."

Andrew Scipione has witnessed unthinkable human acts. However, he chooses to ignore the pain that those horrible memories bring him, as he knows it's his choice to allow it to affect his overall health. I believe that we can all learn a lesson from one of Australia's top former cops and leaders.

If Andrew can do it, so can we!

As previously mentioned, another of my most memorable conversations on my podcast was with a ninety-four-year-old Auschwitz survivor, Dr. Edith Eger. Dr. Eger is truly an inspirational human being. Her mindset and outlook toward life, even at the age she is now, is one to behold and to adopt into our own lives. I had such a deep and meaningful conversation with this lady, who has written her own two bestselling books titled *The Choice* and *The Gift*. *The Gift* reached the status of being a *New York Times* bestseller, which is an outstanding achievement.

During our conversation, I asked her about mindset and how she has been able to remain so positive despite having gone through one of history's most vile atrocities.

Her response was, "I remember when I was in the cattle cart and my mother said to me, 'We don't know where we are going or what is going to happen, but just remember no one can take away what is in your mind. That is our choice.'"

Dr. Edith's story is certainly one that everyone should learn more about. She is an authentic example of a young-minded, present woman who knows that even though we are unable to change the past, we can change our attitude, as that's our choice. This is even more inspirational given that Dr. Edith has experienced indescribable acts of inhumanity. Dr. Edith chose to rise above all the pain, all the hate, and all the distain the Nazi party had for her and the Jewish people. Dr. Edith teaches that, if you are struggling with mental illness, you *can* become a conqueror in your life. It starts with *a choice*.

Many men and women *choose* to play the victim because it's easier than facing the pain head-on. I know this to be true because for years I chose the victim mentality, and it became this vicious cycle of personal mental and emotional abuse. I made it worse for myself. The more I cried out for attention, the worse my mindset became.

How Can I Apply Choice in My Life?

The first step in working through your mental health issues is to understand that it's your choice to believe that this is all life has to offer you right now. You are limiting yourself to greater things that could bring you fulfillment, joy, peace, and meaning. But you have chosen to stay in that negative place where you are right now.

It's your choice to believe the lies floating around in your head. It's your choice to play the victim—and I want you to ask yourself: how does playing the victim make me feel?

I know that it made me feel terrible and took me away from living a life filled with happiness and contentment. I was constantly relying on the opinions of others to make myself feel "better."

I need you to understand that your life is *precious*. Don't take it for granted. You don't have to stay on the current path you've chosen with your mental health. Don't allow ego and pride to tell you otherwise—take control over your choices. It's time for you to make the best choice possible and face up to the pain. I want you to know there are far more greater things waiting for you on the other side of that pain.

Here's what has helped me over the years, and I hope that it will help you too. This isn't anything new, and you've probably heard or read it recommended a million times before, but it does work!

Grab a pen and paper and write down all the lies you believe right now. Now cross them out one by one and change them from a negative into a positive.

For example:

1. From the lie of "I'm not worth it" to the truth of "I know I am worth it."
2. From the lie of "I'm ugly" to the truth of "I'm beautiful." Not because someone has said so but because I believe God made me to be beautiful inside and out.
3. From the lie of "I will never be loved" to the truth of "I am loved, and I am worthy of love."

If you make the choice to start writing down each lie you come across and change them into positive truths, I guarantee that you will start to feel better. If you get stuck, ask someone you love and trust for help.

Remember that in this instance, silence is not golden.

If you know someone that is struggling with mental health issues right now or they just need a boost in life, you also have a choice to ask them if they are okay. Never be afraid to ask if someone is okay because you never know who needs help.

> A tall, blond-haired man is standing at the edge of a bridge looking down toward the rocks below. It's a busy highway, but no one stops to check if this man is okay. While this man is contemplating suicide, he hears a voice in the distance. He turns his head to

oe that a cab driver has suddenly stopped his car and is now running toward him crying out, *"Don't jump!"*

The cab driver finally reaches the man standing at the edge of the bridge.

The man looks at him with tears in his eyes and says, "Why did you stop?"

The cab driver, who is a short, stocky-looking black man, replies, "Because I don't want you to lose your precious life this way. Now come on down from that ledge and let's talk about what is hurting you."

The man looks down again at the rocky surface below, then he turns and steps down from the edge of the bridge, right into the wide and warm embrace of this random stranger.

The cab driver didn't wake up that morning thinking he'd save someone from committing suicide. The cab driver had a choice to make when he saw the man at the edge of the bridge who looked ready to jump. Like everyone else who made the choice *not* to stop, the cab driver could have kept driving and gone about his day none the wiser. Instead, this kind human decided to stop and try to save the man. He didn't know what had caused the man to want to kill himself; all the cab driver was thinking at that moment was how to help save the man's *precious life*.

You can make the *choice* to help those who need help to get through their pain. All it takes is asking someone whether they are okay.

And you also make the *choice* to believe that today is the day for transformation. You make the choice to start believing that you are worthy of greatness, kindness, love, peace, joy, and happiness. Not because Jarred says so, but because you know so!

A = Acceptance

The year 2019 was a difficult year for me—hands down, it was a year of learning how to *accept* difficult circumstances and to accept that I didn't have to continue to suffer from a negative mindset. Acceptance can only come when you make the choice to move forward in your life with grace and humility.

Part of acceptance is embracing what is and not what will be. The more we focus on what *will be* instead of what *is*, the more we are choosing to run from acceptance. We can't ever control what happens in the future, so why spend so much time worrying about it? It's important to be mindful of the future, but that doesn't mean allowing your mind to think of endless negative possibilities of things that haven't even happened yet.

In 2019, the relationship that I had invested all my time, money, energy, and whole identity into ended. Looking back now, there were a lot of warning signs that it was about to end, but I didn't care to accept that they were there.

I had a conversation with my ex about the what-ifs in life a few weeks before we broke up. She asked me what I would do if we weren't meant to be together in the future. It hurt to hear her ask me that because I had chosen to believe that we were going to be together in the future no matter what. I was determined that nothing would break us apart.

I told her that I didn't like focusing on the what-ifs in life, as they haven't happened, and besides, I wouldn't allow us to break up; I loved her too much.

She then asked me again, but this time she held a more serious tone. I couldn't believe what she was asking me, so I just responded with, "Okay, just say that if we weren't to be together in the future, then I'd need to try and get over you and find someone else."

I didn't realize it then, but what she was trying to get me to understand was that she wanted me to accept the possibility of us not being together in the future, as a way of helping me through what was to come. It was also another huge warning sign that I again chose to ignore.

Toward the end of our relationship, my ex and I went on a two-week break, just so that she could figure out what she really wanted in life. I was a little worried because I had heard that when people went on a break from their partner, they hardly ever got back together. It's funny now because I kept saying to her that I didn't focus on all the what-ifs, yet there I was allowing my mind to think of all the negative what-if scenarios.

For that two-week period, I was utterly miserable. I had just started working in real estate, so I wasn't able to show any emotions, and I couldn't really go to anyone and let them know that I was struggling. But deep inside, I was dying.

Then D-Day happened.

It was a Saturday, and I was at an open home inspection. Nothing was happening around me, so I decided to check my social media, and to my shock I saw that my girlfriend had deleted the photos of us together and changed her relationship status to single. (I know; it's rather shallow to base a relationship on social media.) That was the moment when my mind went to an even darker place.

Sadly, I was so worried about losing her that I didn't show any signs of maturity. I kept trying to message her. I thought of dark, and I mean dark, what-if scenarios—some I can't even repeat.

Straight after I saw the status change, I sent her a very harsh text message. She called me that night to try and explain why she had decided to leave me. I was angry, frustrated, and confused. I didn't want to believe it was real.

If you have ever been through a messy breakup, you know that the hardest part is accepting that it's real. You know the cliched response of: "it feels like a bad dream." And you know why something gets labeled a cliché? Because it's *true*!

I'll speak more about the events leading up to the breakup in a later chapter. But I want to focus on my reaction for a moment. I didn't want to *accept* that the pain I was experiencing was real. I didn't want to *accept* that the woman I loved was no longer going to be "mine" in the future.

Not *accepting* was my *choice*, which I made based on my emotional state at the time. I allowed my emotions to control my self-worth and who I was. I felt like a nobody, like I was never going to be loved again. It was a miracle that I made it home safely after that day.

I haven't really shared the whole story of my attempted suicide with many people before because I was so ashamed of myself. I did eventually open up and share a few short versions of what happened on my podcast. And even then, it was extremely difficult for me to talk about. I had contemplated suicide in the past when I was fourteen and for a brief time when I was fifteen. But I never wanted to go through with it. That is until the compounding events of 2019 happened.

I drove home after a horrible day at work a few weeks after the breakup, crying and screaming in my car from the pain. I felt like my life wasn't going anywhere. I don't like sharing this part, but I will in the hopes it might help someone that is in the same position I was in.

I chose that afternoon as the time to just end it all. I didn't want to deal with the pain anymore, so while driving home, I put my foot down on the accelerator and drove straight for the giant pole at the end of the stretch of road that I was on at around 130 kilometers (eighty miles) an hour. I would drive on this stretch of road every day home from work, so I knew the exact pole I wanted to hit. I had seen enough car crash investigation videos to know that hitting a pole at 130 kilometers an hour would more than likely kill me. And that was my goal.

I can only explain what happened next as a "God miracle moment."

I took my hands off the wheel, which was veering toward where the pole was, but I watched as the steering wheel quickly turned away from the pole (which was on the left-hand side of the road) and made the car head toward the right side of the road. My foot also eased up on the accelerator and it landed on the brake, taking my car to a complete stop on the right hand side of the road. I didn't even feel my foot hit the brake either. I just sat there frozen, trying to gain composure. I turned on my hazard lights so other drivers knew to change lanes and go past me. When I had calmed down, instead of going home, I drove to where my grandy and grandma were buried.

It was truly difficult to accept that I was no longer in a relationship, that I had lost my beloved German Shepherd months before, that I was coping with abuse at work, and that I had almost tried to end my life moments earlier.

When I arrived at the burial site, I turned on the radio to Hope 103.2, a radio station I hardly ever listened to. In that moment, I heard a song played by the band Third Day. The song was called, "I Need a Miracle." To this day, I tear up every time I listen to it. I sat in my car for ages just bawling. I cried out to God and said, "Lord, give me a miracle. Give my life meaning and purpose. Show me who you want me to be and what you want me to do." I didn't hear a voice, nothing special at all—I just felt calm.

When my ex-girlfriend called me the night she broke up with me to explain herself, I was so angry that I wanted to throw a chair out my window. Two things happened that stopped me from throwing that chair out my window. The first was my little puppy Alita walking into the room as I picked up the chair, and she looked at me with her piercing brown eyes and jumped on me.

I decided to put down the chair but I then yelled out a very nasty sentence that I regret saying to my ex-girlfriend. It broke any respect that my ex had for me and destroyed the possibility of continuing a friendship. I was so hurt that all I wanted to do was hurt her back.

The second thing that happened was that after I said the hurtful sentence, I immediately punched a hole in my office wall. That was the last time I ever got angry to that extent. And the hole reminds me why I don't get angry today.

It took me many months to finally accept that she no longer wanted me in her life. I even tried to get her back on several occasions, which didn't work. I just didn't want to *accept* letting her go. I was afraid that if I did let her go, I'd never find anyone else again.

The reason why so many people choose to accept the continued suffering of their mental health is because they have accepted that pain and suffering is inescapable for them.

I once had the opportunity to speak with Marisa Peer, one of Britain's leading experts when it comes to mental health issues and one of the pioneers when it comes to knowing your worth. She has worked with celebrities, CEOs, royalty, and Olympic athletes. But Marisa is someone who has dealt with her own battles in the past.

When I asked her if she had struggled and how she handled it, she said, "Of course I have struggled. When I was growing up, I was the most insecure, self-conscious kid ever. I thought I was hideous. I thought I was stupid. We are born with phenomenal self-belief. Unbelief starts as a kid when people say to them: I love you because you are...cute, funny, good-looking... and what the child starts to think is: Oh, but what if I wasn't cute anymore? Then does that mean I wouldn't be worth anything? It's a great shame that kids have started believing and accepting that it's their fault. It begins a painful lifestyle of believing that you aren't enough."

For me, I had chosen to tie myself down to the pain, and I had also chosen to accept suffering as a normal part of my life. When you suffer with mental health problems, you are like that elephant tied to the rope believing it can't move forward, even when there is nothing really stopping you from healing.

Everyone has mental health ups and downs. Some of us struggle with it more than others. But the only way you are going to truly heal from your pain and suffering is when you *choose to accept* that it's doing you more harm than good and that you can break free.

How Can I Apply Acceptance in My Life?

I once had a conversation with three-time World MMA champion Michael Chandler. This man has achieved some incredible feats in the cage—from most wins in Bellator history, most submission wins in Bellator history, and most knockout wins in Bellator history.

One thing Michael mentioned to me during our conversation was the importance of *accountability*.

We often are fearful of going to someone for advice or help. When we are in such a negative state of mind, one of the worst thoughts is *judgement*. Questions arise: what will he/she think of me if I reveal this secret? Will they still want to be my friend or will they still want to help me?

Accountability is vital when it comes to dealing with acceptance. Michael told me something very interesting, and this is a man who has had the spotlight on him for a long time to perform at such a high level.

He simply said, "You are in charge of your own mental state. You decide whether you will allow others to win over you. Don't blame your state of mind on someone else, either; you are just allowing more room for your own self-defeat."

What Michael told me is true. You are in charge of whether you accept something negative into your life or not.

Imagine that you are in a wrestling match. But your mind is the cage, and your opponent is a negative mindset. We fight and run from the negative mindset for a while, but eventually we get tired. And when we get tired from fighting with this negative mindset, we accept it and allow it to pin us down. The count starts: one, two...will you allow acceptance of your negative mindset to make you tap out and give in? Or will you choose to accept the positives back into your mind? Remember, you can choose at any moment to change your state of mind. You just need to accept that you can.

Stop getting beaten up when you don't have to. We can be our own worst enemies at times. So it's time to start winning at your life and stop fighting for a change—do you agree?

Here are a few key strategies that I implement into my life that have helped me with the hard lesson of acceptance.

1. *Calm your mind*—There are many books written by authors who learned the value of calming one's mind and body. Before an eagle strikes its prey, it needs to be as relaxed and quiet as possible, otherwise its prey will sense it coming and run away. If you are depressed, anxious, and stressed, then think of those negative thoughts as the prey and your mind as the eagle. Steady, relax, and take a deep breath in and out. An eagle will sit high up in the trees looking down at its prey before striking.

Make today the day that you finally steady and calm your mind enough to catch and win against the negative thoughts. Don't allow them to continue running free in your mind. If you miss one day, start over again. Remember: an eagle never quits. An eagle is persistent.

2. *Practice gratitude*—This strategy is the most important one. If you live in a developed, industrialized country, then you are spoiled. We are truly blessed beyond measure, yet for some reason we take many things for granted. There is simply no good excuse for why we shouldn't be more grateful. For those of you who have chosen to accept depression as part of your life (and I know this to be true of me when I was depressed), you aren't practicing gratitude at all. It hurts to soak that in—but it's the truth. When I was depressed, I had chosen to be ungrateful for everything I had. Learn to practice being grateful daily: write down seven things you are grateful for every day. (It doesn't need to be seven; I just write down seven things because the number seven has biblical significance.) It doesn't have to be grand; it can be so small, such as: I'm grateful for my toothbrush and toothpaste to clean my teeth. I mean, how many times do we take for granted the smallest items that make a huge impact on our lives? Gratitude is an attitude that you have a choice to accept or not. It is the only emotion that you can decide at any moment to turn on and off. I know of many individuals who keep gratitude journals. If you don't already have one, try it for yourself and see the incredible difference it makes to your mindset and therefore overall quality of life.

3. *Forgive yourself daily*—I've mentioned this a few times, but we can be our own worst enemies, especially if we are depressed. I learned this strategy from one of

my previous therapists. She asked me to set a reminder on my phone that simply said, "Jay, have you forgiven yourself today?" At first, I thought there was no way I was going to do that. The idea sounded a bit stupid—and I hadn't even tried it. My mind was so polluted with negative thoughts that if there was anything new that remotely resembled positive change, I quickly put a stop to it. What my therapist was trying to get me to understand was that I needed to start building good habits to break the bad ones. Even just doing this one thing was a step in the right direction. Luckily, she eventually convinced me to start doing it. And I saw it more as a good challenge than a bad one. The first few days, I felt strange saying, "Jay, I forgive you for everything you've done and will do." But like with any habit, you soon begin to see changes in your daily life, as well as within your mind. And by doing this, I started to experience positive changes.

4. *Be accountable to someone you trust*—When you choose to be accountable to someone that you trust, you are taking a giant step toward improving your life. I once was so afraid to share my deepest, darkest secrets with someone—even if I loved and trusted them. It was because I had allowed fear to take control of my thoughts, emotions, and feelings for such a long time. It was only when I made the *choice* to *accept* that I needed to change—which took time—that I was able to seek help. Having someone keep you accountable means that it's harder for you to slip back into the negative mindset over and over again. Being accountable to someone makes you stronger—two are always better than one. If you want to change, go to someone and get the help required; it will change your life. It has changed mine.

P = Persistence

If you truly want something to happen, it's not going to just fall at your feet. You've got to go after it.

The same principle is also true with overcoming depression, anxiety, stress, and healing your mind, body, and spirit. If you aren't persistent at removing the negativity out of your life, then you won't be consistent at healing. Consistency is the flow-on effect of your persistence. When you make the choice to accept that you need to overcome your depression, then being *persistent* is what you use to keep yourself from falling back into the depressed state of being.

When I finally made the choice to overcome my depression and anxiety, I realized that if I wasn't persistent at doing the work daily, then my mind fell back into those negative thoughts again. I found the metaphorical CAP being released, and I started becoming more stressed, anxious, and worried about even the little things in life.

Persistence in part is a mindset of continuing to never waver from what you desire. If you desire to remain in a depressed state, you will be consistent at staying there. This final part of the CAP method is vital to keep yourself free from pain and suffering. It's all about following through with your *choice* not to *accept* all the negatives that are keeping you down.

Persistence is more than just a mindset too—it's about taking action on a repetitive basis! You need to make the choice daily to accept that you are going to keep the CAP tight (in a figurative and metaphorical sense) on all your negative thoughts. Remember: if an eagle isn't persistent in looking for food, they don't eat, and therefore they will starve. When we aren't persistently focusing our attention toward the positive, we are starving ourselves from a fulfilled and happy life.

A good friend of mine recommended a book, Russell Conwell's *Acres of Diamonds*, and I recommend it to you. It's a perspective shifter for sure. In the book, there's an analogy of two people, each digging for their own diamond. There's an illustration depicting both diamonds at different positions in the ground. It also shows the first person only an inch away from reaching a massive diamond, then giving up and walking away. The second person keeps digging and digging until they finally strike the diamond. That's persistence in having the will and mindset to keep on going no matter what! Nothing is going to move you away from achieving what you want.

If you want to truly overcome the dark place you are currently stuck in, make the *choice* to *accept* that you need to change and *persistently* work hard at changing daily. The change is bringing the positives back into your life not every so often, but every day!

And don't ever give up!

How Can I Apply Persistence in My Life?

All three steps of the CAP method can be difficult if that's how you see it, even though the method is relatively simple at its core. Making a choice to step through pain is hard, especially when you are wrestling with acceptance. Persistence is equally tough because it involves the actions you take to either improve your life or not. And actions take time and the will to carry them out. It also requires work—and how many of us can say we like work? I'll be the first to put up my hand and say no. Yet I'm always working. Why? Because it's good to work at what is good.

Daily, I make the choice to accept that persistence is the key to achieving the things that I want. I want to be happy, healthy, and live an abundant life with my friends and family around me. So for me to achieve these goals, I need to be persistent at working toward this daily. This may involve being of service to others and not just myself, learning new things, forgiving myself, and practicing gratitude—all the strategies I have mentioned above.

It only stops when you make the choice for it to stop.

You may be wondering if I ever struggled with being persistent and keeping my consistency going. Yes, of course I have. I believe we all have those moments. But that's just it—they are only moments. We decide how long they last.

One of my favorite Bible verses is from Psalm 118, verse 24: "This is the day the Lord has made; we will rejoice and be glad in it."

It comes back to accepting gratitude into your life—I work hard daily at persistently telling myself seven things I'm grateful for. The first is always being grateful for the fact I'm still alive.

Remember that you are forever valued and loved, and you can and will achieve great things in your life. When you do finally decide to make the choice to accept that you can change your negative mindset to the positive and persistently work toward keeping yourself there, you will have a far greater and more fulfilled life as a result.

Persistence is one of the most important keys to living a successful and fulfilled life.

You've got this! You don't have to stay on the ground like everyone else. You can soar...just like an eagle was made for.

So, will you make the choice to soar out of your mental health issues?

CHAPTER 6

The Addiction Condition

Addiction: The Fact or Condition of Being Addicted to a Particular Substance or Activity

Before I begin this chapter, I want to mention that I am no expert on addiction—although I have struggled with it for most of my life. This chapter is very raw for me to share, and the reason why I'm going so deep is that I want all who are reading this to learn from my personal experience with battling addiction. I believe that there is great value in being vulnerable to help someone.

Addictions go far beyond just the common forms we often hear about, such as drugs, alcohol, and sex. Addiction is a subject widely spoken about by many doctors and therapists who have studied how addictions affect people's daily lives. I'm certainly no doctor or therapist; however, I have spoken with many well-informed doctors and therapists about the issue of addiction.

The main question everyone seems to ask is: what causes us to become addicted in the first place?

Well, there are many factors involved with people becoming addicted, such as peer pressure, physical and sexual abuse, early exposure to porn, or exposure to drugs and alcohol at an early age. There are also environmental factors associated with addiction. If you are exposed to any of these forms of addiction in the early stages of your development, there is overwhelmingly strong evidence to suggest that you will have an addictive personality in your adult life.

We have yet to fully understand the capabilities of how powerful our brains are. I've spoken with neuroscientists who worked on certain areas of the brain for years and still have lots to learn. What I learned, though, is that there are neurological pathways in our brains that if exposed to repeated forms of addictive substances or behaviors at any stage of life, particularly during puberty, will rewire themselves and often cause us more harm than good. The more addictive behaviors and substances you are exposed to, the more difficult it becomes to break that addiction. I still struggle with controlling my addictions today.

Growing up, I always wanted to learn as many new things as possible. When I was just twelve years old, I made the choice to be exposed to a new world: the world of pornography. Back then, pornography wasn't as big on the internet as it is today, and there wasn't much research done on the effects on the brain, either.

I once got into big trouble for going down the magazine aisle at our local supermarket—there was a plethora of pornographic magazines offered. Mom made it perfectly clear that this aisle was the "dead-man zone." I believe Mom was just trying to protect us for a long as possible from being exposed to what was on display.

In church, we were always told to stay away from porn because it was sinful, and it made God angry. I always strived to be the "good" kid, so I tried to do everything right. Out of fear for what people in the church would think of me, I never questioned the further side effects that porn had on my brain.

Even mentioning the word "sex" was deemed inappropriate and outlawed until you were at least sixteen years old—but even then, no one really spoke about it. It was a rather taboo subject. It's no wonder so many young people are afraid to speak up and get help, especially in most of the conservative Christian circles—which I believe needs to change.

I've spoken with many expert sexologists and therapists about the subject of sex education. It starts with parents understanding that their children need to be educated about sex by parents and not by porn. There is an alarming statistic that if children as young as seven have been exposed to porn, they already have a false sense of reality as to what sex looks like and it is because their minds haven't fully developed yet. As a result, the behaviors they express later on in life could damage their relationships or worse.

I was in class one day and a new kid had just started at school. He was seated next to me, and we instantly hit it off and became good friends. What's more, he had something I didn't. His parents had given him a phone with internet access. Back then, we didn't have iPhones; we had brick phones with small screens. He pulled out his phone during class one day (we always sat at the back of the classroom), and he asked me if I knew what "hardcore" porn was.

I replied, "no," as I had never seen a naked lady in movies before, only on the cover of magazines. So, hook, line, and sinker, I was excited to learn more and asked him to show me a video of hardcore porn.

On his phone, he searched hardcore porn videos and straight away all these video suggestions popped up. It was that easy. He held the phone low so that the teacher couldn't see.

Like a lamb to the slaughter, ignorant that this was going to do me harm, I watched on.

It didn't take long before I was addicted to porn. I couldn't watch it using the internet at home, so I asked my friend to download porn at his place and then give me copies on a USB. This eventually became one of the worst addictions I've ever had in my life. It never really goes away entirely. It is the only addiction whereby you will always remember every single video you ever watched, and you could be triggered at any time, day, or place. I still struggle with the demons that porn has left me with. Trust me, it's a constant battle to keep my mind free of these thoughts. Now, one of the strategies that I use is my CAP method whenever I feel like I might be slipping again. And it's helped me on many occasions! I will speak about some other helpful strategies later in the chapter.

Porn is a multibillion-dollar industry now, and people don't understand the repercussions that porn has on our brains, and therefore life. Porn will literally rewire the neurological pathways in your brain and make you believe that what you are watching is exactly what sex is like. Porn will also teach you about all the things women are "looking for" in a sexual partner. In porn, size does matter, and you are programmed to believe the bigger the better, and that's exactly what a woman needs in her life. You also need to have the six-pack abs along with the chisel jawline. If you don't, then you should feel inadequate.

Porn was responsible for the way I saw myself, because women are looking for a sexy hunk of a man to be with, right?

That is simply not the case at all, but sadly, that's what I believed for many years, and I didn't really know any different.

In 2016, I was so desperate and I thought that if I had the abs and the ripped body, women would want to automatically sleep with me—because that's what happens in porn movies! I quickly discovered that my fantasies from porn were just fantasies and they weren't going to happen in real life. I was shut down by every single woman I approached. And thank God that I was.

So, where is the harm in watching porn?

Well, porn brings to light some of the deepest sexual fantasies that aren't often attained in a real relationship, and it makes women out to be mere objects.

Porn normalizes, and even glorifies, the abuse toward women, and sometimes men. There are whole categories promoting domination, rape, and abuse. Our society doesn't accept sexual abuse, violence, rapists, pedophiles, womanizers, and domestic abuse, but we allow it to be okay in porn!

Porn therefore is linked to the ever-growing issue of sexual abuse in our society. A study done on porn found that over 90 percent of pornographic videos depict sexualized violence. Whether it's by name-calling or just physical aggression, it has all led to supporting violence against men and women. People aren't born violent; we are taught to be violent. Porn conditions us to believe that one partner must dominate the other both consciously and subconsciously to have pleasurable sex.

I soon found conversations with women difficult, as my mind would start wandering off to places that I'm ashamed of admitting. The more I dove into my addiction, the more I found that controlling these urges became an even greater struggle. If you don't see that porn damages relationships, then you need to stop listening to the lies.

I am fully aware that some couples watch porn together and they see no harm in doing that. After all: "Look but don't touch, right?"; "It's fulfilling each of our fantasies"; "We are happy watching porn together"; "Our relationship is better when we watch porn."

However, I have several problems with these statements. The first is: why would you bring certain things into your relationship that ultimately don't serve you both? God said that when you lust after another man or woman, you have already committed the act in your heart and mind. If you are married or in a relationship with someone and you lust after another person's husband or wife, God considers it the same as doing the act in real life, and it is therefore adultery.

In modern vernacular, that's considered cheating. Porn promotes cheating as being acceptable and okay—again, there is no harm if you look but don't touch, right? But I hate to be the one to break the news to you—how can you say that you completely love someone and live in full integrity while you are thinking about someone else in a sexual way, or are lusting after them? Your mind is deceitful and desperately wicked. This so-called "harmless" thing, if allowed to fester and grow, will eventually cause problems. Relationships are built on trust, and porn will sever that trust, believe me.

I understand how some men and even some women need that release, but porn is not the answer. Based on my personal experience, it's not worth damaging your precious mind to the point where it will create issues within your relationships or even your health. Be wiser.

The second problem is that your imagination will often create unrealistic, pleasurable desires and disguise them as perfect-sounding lies. But if left unattained, these lies can leave you feeling unsatisfied, unhappy, unfulfilled, resentful, and will always make you want more.

The third issue I have with porn is that most men and even some women that become addicted to porn think they can fix it when they get into a relationship. That never—and I mean never—happens! You always bring your addiction to porn into your relationship, which is poison and should be treated as such if you want a healthy and meaningful relationship with your partner.

Let me ask you a serious question: if you are addicted to porn, do you want to create meaningful relationships and have a deeper connection with someone? How are you going to do that if you are allowing your addiction to porn control your thoughts?

It's time to get your mind out of the gutter!

But yes, sometimes it's easier said than done, given that we live in such a sexualized world. Everywhere you look now, there is a poster promoting an overly sexualized product or service. We often see a lot of it on TV shows and in films; they glorify sexual content. Why? Because it sells to a mass audience. Content is king, and so is sexual drama—it hooks people in.

But sex appeal sells, so where is the harm if I'm just doing it to make money?

Sadly, these people who drive content like this don't care about the impact that this kind of material has on the minds of our youth. They no longer care about the influence they have; all they seem to care about is money and control.

Children today are looking up to these sex symbols for knowledge and some go as far as to model their whole lives after them. I'm not excused from this at all because I struggled with it too, even into my early young adult life. I didn't realize it at the time, but porn was teaching me how I should act, dress, talk, and think. Porn is an educational platform whether you realize it or not; however, what you are digesting is the wrong form of education. Porn teaches you that it's okay to lie, cheat, steal, abuse, and even lust after another's man or woman.

There is a deep shame that is also attached with being addicted to porn. For many years, I knew that *shame* as my abusive friend. It led me down many dark paths and even contributed to my depression at times.

No one knew about my addiction, and if anyone asked me if I had seen porn before, I just denied it. Let me be very honest: porn also brought forth unhealthy fears. (I also had other unhealthy fears as a result of how I was brought up and made to think actual sex was bad.) The worst fear that I had was being caught. If I got caught, that meant my secret was out in the open and I'd no longer be the goody two-shoes everyone thought I was. I would be forced to get help, even though I thought I didn't need it.

Here is a valuable lesson everyone should learn at some point in life: you can continue to lie to those around you, but the one person you can never lie to is yourself. Eventually, that lie will become so big and so toxic that you can no longer stand to look at yourself in the mirror. Every time I looked at myself in the mirror, all I could see and feel was unworthiness and shame.

I was twenty-one years old when I finally had enough; however, giving up this addiction would prove to be another painful challenge.

Brace for Impact

I had allowed porn to control my thoughts ever since I was twelve years old. When I was twenty-one, I felt it was time to finally take that control back. But taking back control proved difficult at first. I decided to quit cold turkey. The first two weeks were unbearable. I felt like I was a drug addict needing his next fix, and yes, I displayed most if not all of the signs of withdrawal. I thought I was going stir-crazy at times. My mood changed dramatically, and people started to ask what was wrong with me. And, of course, I couldn't share what was really going on, so I just lied about it. It's interesting that when you form one bad addiction, it's easy to create another one.

In 2016, I became addicted to a sport called CrossFit. I was working out seven days a week, sometimes two times a day. CrossFit took over my life just like porn did. I lived and breathed CrossFit. Everything seemed to revolve around this sport, which had just started to become popular. The reason why I loved CrossFit was because of the athletic struggle and pain I felt during and after a workout. It was also a good way for me to channel all that built-up nervous sexual energy I had from trying to quit porn. It wasn't long though before I went spiraling back into my old ways. I didn't grasp or understand the importance of balance in my life.

When I started CrossFit, I was a healthy, lean seventy-two kilograms (158 pounds) of pure muscle. After about two months, I had dropped down to sixty-eight kilograms (149 pounds) and my energy levels weren't there anymore. I didn't understand the importance of proper nutrition and I wouldn't eat enough to refuel my body or keep my muscle mass. The more I trained, the better I thought I looked, and I kept telling myself it was okay to keep on doing what I was doing. I also listened to people around me saying how good I looked. So I kept on doing it.

I ate a one-kilogram bag of spinach a day, and I cut out most carbs and fats. I just stuck to small amounts of chicken breast, cheese sauce with spinach—sounds boring, doesn't it? That's because it was. The more I cut out foods because I thought they were "unhealthy" and that I'd get "fat," the more restrictive I became. To make matters even worse, I exercised harder and for longer. Some days, I exercised for at least two and a half hours.

One afternoon, I got injured during my workout. I hurt both of my shoulders to the point where I couldn't lift the weights above my head anymore. This sucked, but I kept doing other workouts instead and didn't allow my body any time to rest. I was so fixated on the fact my body would heal quickly that I just kept at it. Financially, I was spending money like crazy and not saving anything. The gym was by far my first priority above all else, but I couldn't keep up with the payments. I had to eventually leave the place I loved.

However, I needed to keep my addiction alive, and since I didn't have the money for the gym anymore, I thought, *well, it's free to run out in the fresh air*—so that's what I did. I started running, and before long, what started out with just thirty minutes each day eventually become two hours every morning for six days straight. Plus, I did a twenty-to-thirty-minute high-intensity workout after the run. I also mixed it with a goal of one thousand push-ups a day, which I achieved on a frequent basis for five months. I had no days off with my push-ups.

During this whole time, I went back to watching porn, and I thought if I could achieve the six-pack abs, then maybe girls would want me. After all, that's what the porn videos indoctrinated me to believe I needed to have. It was a very shallow way of looking at my life; I didn't value myself enough, and I was chasing all the wrong ideas and beliefs. Looking back now, it is sad to think that that is what I believed. But as they say: hindsight is 20/20.

The more I ran, the more I felt free and away from my problems.

For over a year, I kept feeding my exercise and porn addictions, when other really bad habits/addictions began to form. I developed a severe eating disorder as a result from my addiction to exercise. I was now at sixty-five kilograms (143 pounds) and only about 8 percent body fat. My hormones were running wild; I developed frequent mood swings, fatigue, and at the same time I noticed that I didn't have a sexual drive anymore. I thought this was great because I no longer had the same desire to watch porn.

I honestly felt so good about losing one addiction that I failed to see the other addictions that had taken over. My eating disorder was now in control of every area of my life. I had people tell me that my weight was too low and that I needed to gain more. But do you think that I listened? Of course not.

What eating disorders do is keep you in a complete state of denial. When you look in the mirror every morning, all you see is a fat and hideous person needing to gain more control over what you eat to lose weight faster. Even if you aren't fat, you believe that you are. (Or it could be the other way around for some people.) An eating disorder is all mental, but it affects the physical, spiritual, and emotional aspects of your health.

I understand that there are many people who struggle with eating disorders, and once you have it, it never goes away. Over time, you just learn how to manage it along with your addiction (or addictions) and views toward food.

For those of you who are struggling with an eating disorder (or disorders)—whether it's binge eating, spitting and chewing food (this was what I did frequently), vomiting, or undereating (I also did this too)—there is hope and a way out for you. Please don't ever beat yourself up about your addiction, please don't be afraid to ask for help, and please don't keep it a secret! I hope that my story will again be helpful and a warning and reminder to those who are struggling.

The Broken Struggle

Toward the end of 2017, I went on a cruise with my family, and I hated it. My mind was always buzzing, and I felt annoyed to be kept in such a confined space. I was always up at 4 a.m. and ran up fourteen flights of stairs to the top deck and then ran for about one hour and forty-five minutes.

I was also still losing weight...and fast; I had dropped down to a staggering sixty-two kilograms (136 pounds) by this point.

Every morning when I first got up, I spent at least thirty minutes on the toilet in excruciating pain. I didn't really think anything of it and didn't bother telling my mom about it either.

When we got home from our cruise, I started feeling worse. I had constant diarrhea, and the pain each time I went just kept growing—it was like nothing I had ever experienced before in my life. I also started getting pain in my kidneys again because they had become severely dehydrated from all the running, along with the diarrhea. I had no idea that my kidneys weren't retaining any of the fluid that I was drinking. My skin was now yellow, and my mom kept telling me that I should go to the doctor to get checked.

After constant nagging from Mom, I finally went to see the doctor. I had blood tests done, as well as an x-ray and ultrasound. When my doctor examined the results, she said that there was a major blockage in my bowel, and I needed to immediately rehydrate my kidneys—so off to the hospital I went!

Being admitted into a ward drove me almost to the point of insanity, but physically, I had almost given up from all the pain. Do you know what I was doing while in the hospital though? Yes, that's right, I kept doing my push-ups secretly in the bathroom. My mind was clearly not right at all.

That's the problem with people with an eating disorder and an addiction to exercise: nothing, and I mean nothing, but death itself will stop you. At least, that was the truth for me during this time.

The first hospital trip was by far the worst. Yes, you read correctly—this was only the first visit. And while there, I saw several specialists, including my nephrologist, who looked after my kidneys.

This was where all the dignity I had cherished went before I could blink! On further investigation, my doctor found that my bowel was blocked by fecal matter, and it was like a brick. (Have a guess how that happened? Yep, all the spinach, cheese sauce, and lack of fiber in my diet!) And the first thing that had to be done was unblock it, which wasn't a pleasant experience at all. They certainly didn't use a plunger! No, it was far worse than that.

They gave me these tablets to take that were meant to dissolve the fecal matter. And when that didn't work, I was given the same fluids that patients who are preparing for a colonoscopy are given. This fluid is meant to clean you right out. But sadly, that didn't work either, so the nurses went back to the drawing board.

And I didn't like what they came back with!

The nurses said that they'd stick this oval-shaped tablet right up my rectum. The tablet would then circle around the fecal matter, trying to soften it. Once that had happened, I needed to be prepared for the explosion of a lifetime—to put it candidly.

According to the nurses, it would only take about ten minutes. I felt so sorry for the nurse who had to do this. Unfortunately, it didn't work the first time, so we had to try again. Second time: nothing happened. It was clear that my doctor needed to come up with something else!

The next "solution" was to give me double the dosage of fluids that patients who are preparing for a colonoscopy are given.

I was hoping and praying that this would work because I was in so much pain and I didn't want the toilet to continue being my best friend.

When you're in the hospital, there is no such thing as dignity—and mine was long gone now. A small price to pay for my addictions. (This was just one of the many prices I had to pay because of my addictions.)

Hours went by and still nothing was working. The fluids didn't work again. However, I was sick to death of being in hospital. So, when the pain eventually began to ease at the end of day three, the doctor said that I could go home if I felt better by the end of the day. And that's exactly what happened. By the end of day four, I went home.

When I arrived home that night, my dog Joy wouldn't leave me alone. She could clearly smell that something was still not right with me, and so she followed me around for the next few days; she didn't eat, either. Joy actually saved my life.

It was a Saturday morning, and I woke up feeling terrible. To cut a long story short, I ended up at my doctor's and she told Mom to take me straight back to the hospital. This time, however, I was to see a gastroenterologist.

Once we arrived, we needed to wait for a few hours in the emergency room before anyone saw us. I eventually saw a triage doctor, who ran all these tests; he even stuck his finger up my backside for no reason at all. This doctor gave Mom and me the creeps. I literally wanted to run home.

Four hours later and I was finally admitted into a ward. I had my own room with a great view; it almost felt like I was in a five-star hotel. However, this hospital trip was very different from the last.

At 8 p.m. Saturday night, the gastroenterologist walked into my room, and the first thing he said was, "Jarred, I have forty-five years of experience in this profession, so you'll be in the most capable hands."

He then went over my scans and blood results that had been done in the previous hospital, as well as all the blood work from the last week. He asked me a lot of questions, some I can't even remember, as there were that many.

To my pleasant surprise, he doesn't stick his fingers up my backside at all, which to me, earned him extra brownie points. I even told him what the triage doctor did, and the specialist was a bit surprised. That was the first time he had ever heard of a triage doctor feeling for any fecal matter directly.

I said, "Doctor, it was a massive invasion of my privacy, and he didn't even ask, he just said he was going to do it."

The specialist assured me that that would never happen again while he was looking after me, and that he'd get to the bottom (no pun intended there) of what happened. He also apologized on behalf of this triage doctor. (I seem to have a bad history with triage doctors, don't I!)

The specialist then explained his solution for my painful problem. He wanted to triple the dosage of fluids that I had previously been given. Now, I don't know if you are reading this and you've had to prepare for a colonoscopy before, but it's not fun at all. You can't eat and you can't sleep because you need to be constantly going back and forth to the toilet every couple of minutes.

For me, it was soon to be every second.

The next morning, I began my treatment.

My nurse came in and asked, "Are you ready, Mr. Fantom?"

I replied jokingly, "I don't have a choice, do I?"

The first night was horrific. I was going back and forth to the toilet constantly; my body was aching like you wouldn't believe. I felt like I didn't have the energy to keep going, but there was no turning back now.

Daybreak and I was no closer to being free from this horrific pain. To make matters worse, I couldn't sleep, and I was downright miserable. And there was nothing good on TV apart from the cooking shows—funny enough, that is where I learned how to cook. (There is always a silver lining to everything!)

The specialist didn't see me on day two; however, he did prescribe me continual triple doses of that horrid substance. He was determined that eventually the blockage would give up. I wasn't so sure myself; he clearly hadn't met a Fantom before. Fantoms are known for not doing things the normal way.

On day three, I saw the specialist and gave him an update on my progress. The pain started to ease the night before, and I was up at 4 a.m. walking up and down the aisles with my cannula still in my arm. I had to take the pole with the fluid bag attached everywhere I went. All the nurses thought I was crazy and should have been in bed sleeping. I said that I was feeling a bit better, and I needed to burn off some stress by walking. (Another lie, even though I was in so much pain and should have learned a big lesson from this, but alas, nothing was breaking me—so it seemed.)

The specialist prescribed me some more of that horrible stuff again just to make sure there wasn't a blockage we "might" have missed. I have always said: "It is better to be safe than sorry."

So, I had to endure one more day of torture. However, by the end of the day, I was feeling empty. I hadn't eaten for the past three days, and I was starving! My dad came to see me that afternoon with some of my favorite snacks: a Crunchie bar, a KitKat, and M&M's.

I was at the hospital for a total of four and a half days. My final night was more pleasant, thankfully I was allowed to eat. I can't tell you how good it was to eat something and keep it down.

On my final night in hospital, I ended up speaking to one of the nurses about why I was in hospital in the first place. She said, "You're young, Jay; you shouldn't be here."

She was 1,000 percent right. I was young, and I shouldn't have gone through the amount of pain that I did. I shouldn't have been sitting in that hospital bed. Yet, there I was at sixty kilograms (132 pounds) now, skin and bone, with no energy and feeling miserable. I did this to myself.

How did I get here in the first place? It all started way back with my addiction to porn—and I just allowed it to go on and on and on. When the nurse left, I began bawling. I didn't sleep for the rest of the night; instead I sat in the chair next to the window, waiting for the sun to come up.

The specialist came in on my final day to explain the next steps of my recovery process. He said that I needed a colonoscopy so he could have a proper look around and determine what was the cause of the blockage in the first place. (My simple diet!) He explained that I had to go through the preparation process again, which I wasn't too happy about. The date of the procedure, however, would be later that same year.

I thanked him for looking after me, and he said, "You're the sort of person that bottles things up inside. This can affect your bowel. Whenever you find yourself in a stressful situation, remember to breathe. If you remember to breathe, life will be all right." He then shook my hand and walked out of the room to see his other patients.

Change?

A few months after I left hospital, I had my colonoscopy (which didn't show anything major except that I had irritable bowel syndrome), and so I started on my road to healing.

However, I became sick again.

After weeks of severe pain, I had incredible sugar cravings to the point where I'd sit on the couch with a two-liter tub of ice cream and "it wouldn't even touch the sides" (a term my dad uses when someone doesn't get full or gain weight from eating junk food). This may seem like a dream for a lot of people, but it was far from fun. My body wasn't retaining any nutrients at all, which meant that I had no energy for anything. And I was always angry. I didn't fit my clothes, and I was craving food constantly.

I was living like this for months without any sign of change. And truth be told, even though I was miserable, I liked being the size that I was. (fifty-three kilograms and only 3 percent body fat) However, my mom's persistence that I see a doctor, yes, yet again, prevailed. This time, instead of seeing a regular doctor, I went to see a naturopath—but I was skeptical about how she could help me.

I sat in her office with a proud attitude, like I didn't need to be there. And the naturopath clearly sensed that I wasn't happy, but she still proceeded to ask me all kinds of in-depth questions. I answered them to the best of my reluctant ability, and toward the end, she said that I had all the signs of the horrible bacterial syndrome called SIBO (small intestinal bacteria overgrowth).

Treating SIBO is an extremely difficult, expensive, long, and painful process. I started eating garlic cloves without anything to go with them: nature's natural medicine. And when the garlic didn't work, she put me on a more potent medicine. I can't remember exactly what the substance was, but it did the trick. Taking the medicine wasn't the hardest part—it was having to change my mindset toward food and my entire diet.

Eventually, after weeks of taking the medication and having to drastically change my mindset toward food, my body started to recover. I stopped eating so much sugar and went on a mostly meat-and-vegetable diet. I put all my cooking skills to good use during that time. I started researching and reading books from certain doctors and health food professionals, such as Dr. Steven Gundry, Jo Whitton, Dr. Will Cole, and Dr. Josh Axe, about the importance of having the right foods in my diet.

The more I cut out certain bad food groups, the better I felt. The health food advice that seemed to catch my eye and interest me the most was Dr. Steven Gundry's work on the plant paradox. The way Dr. Gundry spoke about lectins in our microbiome fascinated me. I decided to try his diet for several weeks, and it honestly transformed my entire system. Not only did I feel great, but I gained a healthy weight back. I no longer had IBS, and my SIBO had completely dissipated.

To this day, I still follow Dr. Gundry's diet, and I highly encourage anyone that is struggling with their gut health to get his books. I also read Jo Whitton's cookbook, as well as her recipes online and decided to try some of them too. (I still make her recipes to this day.) I believe that life is about finding balance with what we eat. There are so many amazing foods out there to try. But please don't be like me and go overboard with everything. Learn from my mistakes—you can be better! You should do better! Be better!

If this also interests you, I highly encourage consulting your healthcare professional first, and then doing your own research—know what's out there and get familiar with what will work for your body—and do this all *before* trying any drastic diet changes. There are far too many diets and diet fads out there. So, be careful, seek the right medical advice, know your body, and don't go to the extreme.

I am also proud to say that I have been able to overcome my porn addiction while also managing my eating disorders and addictions to food and exercise.

How?

Well, for porn, I needed to remove myself from the temptations. That meant putting a protective blocker on my computers, phone, and any electronic device with internet access.

The next thing that I did was see someone (a therapist) who I trusted and respected and who I felt wouldn't judge me. She listened to my story and acknowledged the pain I had felt for such a long time. She gave me clear insights and sound wisdom into how to better manage my behaviors moving forward. Whenever I feel like I'm being triggered, I blink twice and breathe in and out through my nose until I feel that thought going away. She also helped me practice quickly replacing those thoughts with new ones while I was breathing in and out.

I also read Bible verses now and I meditate on them every single day.

Another good thing to remember is having someone to keep you accountable. (I've mentioned the importance of accountability in an earlier chapter.) Iron sharpens iron, and if you want to keep your addictions at bay, then having someone you love and trust there to support you will build your strength back up. You aren't going through this alone.

Try these strategies for yourself. They work! You can also use the CAP method if you want. I like having many strategies available to me because that helps build my confidence and sharpen my resilience. If you do fall, pick yourself back up. Don't stay down!

Today, my mindset toward health has never been better. I do my best to eat a balanced diet every day—I'm human, so I do have my moments. I haven't watched porn since I was twenty-two. It's so much more sustainable when you look at food as your friend and not as your enemy. When you struggle with eating disorders, porn addiction, exercise addictions, or even food addiction, you have no idea what the word "balance" really means. Being healthy starts in your mind first; work toward finding the right kind of balance for you. I learned the hard way—not only physically but mentally, spiritually, emotionally, and financially—from my addictions and eating disorders.

We all have a choice whether we want to take care of our bodies, minds, and spirits that we have been given. You can continue to stay where you are right now and even go backward with your health, or you can *choose* to *accept* that you don't need to stay there in pain and suffering, and you can *persistently* work toward finding balance and being healthy.

What choice will you make?

CHAPTER 7

The Sink-or-Swim Method

Everyone Wants to Swim Without First Learning How to Sink

What would you rather do: sink or swim?

Of course, many people will say "swim." I mean, who wants to sink or even experience the feeling of sinking? But what if I told you that if you want to swim, you've got to learn how to sink first, and that you will never truly stop having sinking moments along the journey of life?

On January 18, 2019, my family had to make the extremely difficult decision to put our beloved German Shepherd of eleven years, Joy, to sleep. Even writing this makes me so emotional. Joy was one hell of a fighter; she was resilient even after going through endless amounts of surgeries for bacteria that was growing in her ear. It became so bad at times that it almost killed her.

I remember the day of Joy's passing like it was only minutes ago. Joy had started to deteriorate with her health, and we all saw that she was in extreme pain. It was early in the morning when we called the vet to say that it was time. The vet told us to spend the whole day with her and keep her as calm as possible. Knowing that you're going to put your loved one to sleep is downright painful!

We took Joy Joy (as we called her) for her final car ride. My older brother Nathan had to carry her to the car, as her back legs weren't working that well. She looked so sad in the car, but also at peace. When we got to McDonald's for her favorite treat, it hit me that this was the last time we are taking Joy out for ice cream. I honestly don't know what is worse: knowing that it's the last time, or not knowing and dealing with the aftershock.

When the vet arrived that night, Joy clearly knew what was coming. She hid under my desk, which she used to do whenever she was afraid. We had to pull her out and bring her into the lounge room. Even then, she kept on fighting as hard as she could. The vet told us what would happen and that it would be quick and painless for her. We all gathered around her, and as we said our final goodbyes to our special bundle of Joy, the tears wouldn't stop flowing.

Watching the life go from someone you love is a special but awful moment. It's a sinking moment of despair. I held onto Joy's paw and wouldn't let go. Tears just kept on coming.

My dad cried out, *"It's not fair!"*

I cried even harder in response.

For anyone who has owned a dog or pet and gone through this kind of traumatic experience, you'll know of the pain I'm speaking about.

The next morning, I got up and went for a run; I couldn't see two feet in front of me as tears kept blinding me. I ran past a man walking his German Shepherd (I know, of all the days!). The dog obviously could sense that something wasn't right, so she pulled her owner toward me. I was a mess, and the dog licked my hands and I knelt down and gave her a big hug. The owner of the dog asked if I was okay.

I told him what had happened the night before, and he said something that I will never forget, "She will forever watch over you, my friend, and she will always protect you. Her legacy will live on through you and the stories that you share of her. The joy doesn't stop because she is gone. I don't think she would have wanted that."

This was a man who barely knew Joy, but from the way I spoke of her, he got it.

This was just the start of what I now call "the year of sinking."

Not only did I experience the painful breakup with my girl-friend, but my work life also began to suffer.

On my very first day as a real estate agent, my boss asked me to show a property to a prospective buyer. I couldn't believe it!

I showed up to this brand-new property alone, waiting for the buyer to arrive. The buyer was this sweet older lady with a gentle demeanor. She clearly could tell that it was my first day; I must have looked drastically nervous. She smiled at me and asked me easy questions. We ended up just talking for about twenty minutes, not about the house but why I was in real estate and where I was from.

When I locked up the house, I thought, *thank you, God, that is over!* Then got in my car and took a deep breath. I had sur-vived my first private property inspection.

However, from then on, I was thrown further into the deep end and told to either sink or swim. My second property sale was a huge *sinking* moment. This one particular unit hadn't been sold at auction, which meant that we kept doing open inspec-tions until either it sold, the vendor opted out of the contract, or the contract expired and the vendor didn't renew it. This was the second open weekend for the unit after the auction when it passed in, and I was assigned to show it to potential buyers.

At the start of the inspection, there weren't many interested buyers, but it began to pick up toward the end. (That seemed to be a trend while I was in real estate—more people showed up while we were about to close than when we were open.) This young couple arrived, and they loved the unit. They even asked what the next stages were to purchase the property. Unfortunately, though, there was a miscommunication with the deal, and this couple almost lost this unit (their "dream unit") to another buyer.

I won't go into what exactly happened, but because of what happened, I felt like quitting. I got verbally abused by the mother of the girl wanting to purchase the unit. I was accused of ruining this young couple's dream. And not to mention the verbal abuse that I copped from my boss as well.

I was sinking farther into the darkness of deep water with no sign of the light at the surface. Even though my boss came through with that particular transaction, I still felt horrible and kept thinking that maybe I wasn't cut out for real estate. Little did I realize there were far more sinking moments to come in 2019, and this was just the beginning.

There was another property that had passed in at auction, and the owners wanted a particular amount but the market value for that property didn't match it. Buyers weren't prepared to fork out the amount the owners wanted. This property had been on the market well before I had joined the company.

One day, I decided to do some research to see if there was a certain problem that deterred developers from investing in this property, and if there was, to see if there was a strategy to overcome this problem. We actually had more interested developers than regular buyers due to the size of the block. So I called up the energy company and the local council, and I got information regarding future developments in that area. I then passed that information along to my boss, thinking that I had done the right thing and shown some initiative.

My boss, however, wasn't happy and started to give me a stern lecture about how I shouldn't have wasted so much time on this, how I was wrong, and how my initiative could have cost him a great deal of money. Some of his final words were, "Don't waste your time on a dead duck," which meant don't waste your time on something that won't ever sell, when there are other, more alive "ducks" (properties) to sell on the market.

I have said this as well to many high-level businessmen and women on my podcast, but this was one of the worst pieces of advice I'd ever heard.

The reason why was because he was telling me to give up trying to sell the property and focus my attention on other properties instead, as I didn't have the same level of experience that he did to get that kind of property sold. And after this conversation, I felt like I was sinking further toward the bottom of the ocean. That's how he made me feel.

When my boss left, I just got up from my desk, walked outside to where my car was parked, got in, and screamed at the top of my lungs. I felt more frustration and anger than sadness. This wasn't the first time my boss had given me a harsh lecture and made me feel worthless. There were many—and I mean many—times before this where the mental abuse was insane. I even dreaded going into work out of fear over the next thing my boss might say to me.

I had a second phone, and I was constantly on edge wondering whether the phone would ring or whether there would be a text message from my boss. I didn't know when my boss was going to erupt again. It wasn't a healthy way to live, that's for sure.

When the property sold for nearly the amount the owners were after, they asked me to come to their home for a chat. I didn't know what they were going to say to me, but I went.

The owners welcomed me and asked me to sit at the kitchen table. Firstly, they thanked me, and then they went on to explain why they decided to sell despite the price not being exactly what they wanted.

The husband said, "Jay, we saw how hard you worked every single weekend you were here; you kept us all updated; you showed kindness to everyone that came through, and I want you to know that that doesn't go unnoticed. Your boss was just yelling the whole time he was here about how the offer was the best we would get, blah, blah. We all spoke as a family, and we all agreed that it was because of your hard work that we decided to take the offer and sell below what we wanted."

The owners had no idea how I was feeling during this moment, but this gave me renewed energy.

That sinking feeling I had been experiencing for so long was horrible. But you learn more while you're sinking than you ever will while swimming. All those hard times that you had or are having—they are good for you. In the moment, it's hard to realize because pain often controls our emotions and thoughts. You don't learn anything good when life is going great for you. For example, I never learned anything worthwhile when I was succeeding in real estate, when I had all my sales.

I once spoke with Byron Katie, the bestselling author of multiple books including one of my favorites, *Loving What Is*. I asked her the same question I asked you at the beginning of this chapter—what would you rather: sink or swim?

And her answer was: to sink. She said, "I think people should get comfortable with sinking."

Allow that to process through your mind for a moment. She didn't say get comfortable with swimming, she said get *comfortable* with *sinking*.

The more we become comfortable with sinking, the better it will be for us. Instead of fighting the failures, the pain, the pressures, and hardships, let go for a moment and watch the beauty that will begin to unfold in your life.

I understand that many people feel like they are drowning instead of sinking—but there is a difference. Drowning means you have given up, and essentially, I equate it to death. Sinking means there is still hope for you. It means that you haven't given up—you've accepted what is in your life whether it's painful or not, and you have chosen to embrace it all.

Byron Katie also said during our conversation, "I want it all, and I'm in for the ride." She also used this amazing analogy of when she drinks water and it goes down the wrong pipe. You get that horrible feeling of sinking and choking on the water at the same time. But when the water eventually comes out, you feel excellent! If you take anything away from the sink or swim method, take away Byron Katie's advice. Be excited when the failures and pain come and enjoy the ride, because no matter how bumpy it gets, it will be worth it all. Don't give up!

Keep on soaring.

CHAPTER 8

The Mustard Seed

Failure Is Just Another Way God Is Able to Redirect Us Back to Him and Then Strengthen Our Faith

I believe that this is the most important chapter in my book. What I am about to share with you is the difference between eternal *pain* or eternal *peace*. I haven't shied away from sharing that I am a person of faith or how I was raised in a conservative Christian household. Now, I can understand that some people don't believe in God or that faith even exists. For me, I know that God and faith are very real, and I have lived and experienced it. My faith in God is my guiding light through this crazy, dark world. Each time that I have failed—and believe me, there have been far more than I can count—God has used those failures to not only redirect my attention back toward him, but also to grow my faith.

For those who don't believe in God, ask yourself why not. Look around you: there would have had to have been a creator for all of this. Did you know that your entire body is so intricately detailed that scientists are still researching our body and how it works? That just boggles my mind thinking about how special we all are. Did you know that even though twins look the same, their DNA code is still different, and their fingerprints are different too? How amazing is that?!

Can you imagine giving up something you love dearly and giving it to someone you hate, or they hate you, but you still give what you love to them anyway? How would you feel? That is called "love." And it's exactly what Jesus did for all of us when he died a painful death on the cross. God loved us so much that he made a way for us to be with him forever. He conquered death and provided a way for all that have faith and trust in him to live forever. Many people, past, present, and even future, hate or will hate God and have chosen or will choose to reject him. But Jesus still willingly gave himself for you, for me, and for the people who are still yet to come.

God speaks about having faith the size of a "mustard seed." Have you seen how big a mustard seed is? It's tiny!

Faith itself is so simple, and God even speaks about having childlike faith in order to believe and trust in him. The reason for this is because childlike faith is pure and real. Children's minds aren't tainted by false doctrines and teachings that cause doubt and unbelief to plague their minds.

I heard a story of a little girl who had faith big enough to move mountains. When I tell this story, it gives me goose bumps.

A little girl who was living in a large home for orphans was awoken suddenly in the middle of the night by crying coming from outside of her room. While rubbing her eyes, she slowly got out of bed and walked into the living area, only to discover most of the kids in the home gathered around listening to one of the adults speaking. Not knowing what the adult was talking about, the little girl inched closer to the group and sat down next to one of the other orphans. She asked him what all the commotion was about.

The orphan said in a sad tone, "The authorities told us to evacuate our home because that dormant volcano we are living near is no longer dormant and it could erupt any day now."

The little girl thanked the other orphan for telling her what was happening. She then calmly stood up and walked back into her room, leaving the door wide open.

In this little girl's room was a window overlooking all the mountains, even the large volcano that was about to erupt. The moon was full that night and it gave off this bright white light. The little orphaned girl opened her window and knelt down with her head raised toward the bright sky. She then prayed a very simple prayer: "Heavenly Father, this is my home that you have provided for me. I know that you will always give me what I need, but Father, I'm asking you for the sake of all my fellow brothers and sisters in this home, that you please remove this mountain before us. I love you, in your name I pray. Amen."

The little girl stood back up, closed her window and got back into bed, quickly falling to sleep and feeling at peace.

The next morning, the little girl was shaken awake by another orphan, who yelled, "You have got to see this, quick!" The little girl gingerly got out of bed, and in the corner of her eye she noticed that something was different outside. She walked over to her window, opened it, and to her pleasant surprise, she couldn't see the volcano.

It had suddenly vanished.

That little girl had the faith to believe that God could and would remove a mountain— and God did!

If only you and I were to have the same faith as this little orphan girl did—we would all be able to see God move mountains in our lives.

All we need is some childlike faith.

Faith That Saves Lives

When I was two years and eight months old, I was almost taken to heaven early—this was the first time I nearly died.

Mom told me what happened because events are somewhat sketchy, seeing as I was so young. My older brother and I had been sick with tonsillitis for weeks, and although we were on the mend, we still weren't eating much. Mom called her doctor, who advised her to give my brother and I a *raw* egg in a milkshake.

So that's what Mom did. However, even though the egg wasn't *off*, anything raw from a chicken or egg could have salmonella bacteria all over it. (A little piece of advice for you all: make sure you check the eggs before you use them, especially if they're straight from a farm. If you do buy your eggs directly from the farm, make sure to wash them thoroughly before eating them.)

Later that same night, Nathan became very ill with a high fever. My poor mom was up all night with him. In the early hours of the morning, lightning struck twice this time—I had the same symptoms as my brother, which was (to put them into a gory enough picture for you) buckets of vomit and continual diarrhea. Mom called the doctor and was advised to keep us home to not spread what appeared to be a stomach bug, and he told her to watch us and try to keep our fluids up. If we became worse, Mom was to call an ambulance and get us straight to the hospital.

By lunchtime, Nathan had a febrile convulsion, so Mom decided it was time to call an ambulance. When the ambulance officers arrived, they examined us but told Mom we just had a stomach bug, and we would get over it by the next day. This was very unusual, as paramedics almost never leave children at home so unwell, especially after Mom showed them what we were vomiting up. (Fantoms definitely aren't textbook cases at all!)

It was the Thursday afternoon before Good Friday, and Mom pleaded with them to take us to the hospital, but they refused. When the ambulance officers left, Mom had to call my dad, who was working, to come straight home and take us to the hospital. Nathan and I were both in diapers and on potties in the back seat, with buckets in front of us. (I'm sure those with vivid imaginations can picture what that was like.)

Once we finally arrived at the hospital, we were shocked that there was no one in the emergency waiting room. Mom and Dad carried us straight up to the triage nurse, who ushered us all into the examination room. This was where I greeted the doctor by throwing up all over him. How about that for a first impression!

Both Nathan and I were severely dehydrated. It took quite a few tries to get a cannula into Nathan, but they managed to find a vein. With me, however, it was another story entirely. All my veins had collapsed, and there was nothing the doctors could use to put a cannula in to get my hydration levels back up. They kept feeding me Gastrolyte ice blocks, which I kept throwing back up.

The doctors said to Mom that if things didn't change during the night, they'd have to take me to the operating room to get a cannula in the central vein found in the back of my neck.

Mom and Dad had their friends and the whole church praying for us.

After a few hours, the doctor went over my tiny body again and he managed to find a small vein, which was about the size of a mustard seed, on the top of my foot. They were able to put a fine cannula in, but things were still very touch and go—there was no real guarantee that I was going to make it. Imagine hearing that sort of news. What would be going through your mind?

The next morning, the doctors were able to find a vein in my right arm and give me proper fluids. It was Good Friday, and this date has a great deal of significance for us as Christians because it resembles the crucifixion of Christ.

Mom expressed to me that she was in awe of how God provided everything for us and for her during this time, as she was also seven weeks pregnant with my younger brother Jonathan and wasn't well herself. And because of being pregnant, Mom wasn't allowed to hold us without being gowned, gloved, and masked each time due to cross infection and being at high risk of her losing my younger brother.

We ended up finding out that God provided Christian nurses who not only cared for our health needs, but some cradled Nathan and I while singing our favorite songs to help us sleep, as we were in agonizing pain and crying so much.

The staff commented the next morning on how the whole ward had been settled that night from all the singing. The songs were about Jesus and how we know that God is with us and brings peace to the whole world.

Come Easter Sunday, my brother and I were improving, so the nurses brought in a portable TV and PlayStation so that we could play games or watch films. I can still remember the film we watched; it was *The Lion King*. And the scene that resonated with me, and still does, was when Mufasa said to Simba: "Simba, remember who you are. Remember."

The news came on Easter Sunday that Nathan and I had suffered from salmonella food poisoning and that we both would have died that night had Mom and Dad not brought us to the hospital when they did. I truly believe that the prayers of all those amazing people in my church, and no doubt the Christian nurses, saved my life. It was because of their faith that God saved two little boys from being taken home early. Faith doesn't just have the power to move mountains; it can save lives too!

Do You Trust Me?

It was a Monday morning in November of 2018. I got out of bed feeling a bit light-headed. I didn't think anything of it and just passed it off as having low blood pressure. I still went for a run, and I did my intense CrossFit-style workout.

I came home, cooked something to eat, and did some work. At about 2 p.m. that afternoon, I wanted to close my eyes, as they were becoming sensitive to the light, and it hurt to keep them open. I fell asleep for thirty minutes on the couch, woke up, and moved to my bed, closing all the blinds to be in complete darkness.

My mom came home at 4 p.m. to discover me fast asleep in my bed. This kind of behavior was unusual for me, so she checked my temperature, and it was thirty-nine degrees Celsius (over 102 degrees Fahrenheit)—something wasn't right. At this point in the afternoon, I couldn't see at all—I was completely blind.

Mom decided to drive me down to the local doctor's office. When the receptionist saw me, she took immediate action despite the full waiting room. I was taken into the back and placed on a bed. I didn't have to wait long before I could hear a kind, gentle voice asking me questions. I answered them all to the best of my ability; I had a throbbing headache.

Once the doctor had made her assessment, she told Mom to take me to the hospital right away or she could call an ambulance. The ambulance would have taken twice as long, and the hospital wasn't far from the doctor's office. The doctor feared that I could have the early signs of meningococcal meningitis.

Once again, off to the hospital I went.

We arrived at the hospital and I was taken into the back of the emergency room and placed in a chair, as there were no beds available.

About ten minutes after that, I heard a girl crying; she sounded young. She was wheeled in on a bed by the ambulance officers and placed beside me. Her boyfriend followed and sat in the chair next to her. I could overhear her boyfriend explain to the nurses what had happened. This girl had been through a lot in her young life, and I suddenly felt a sense of compassion for them both, as I could relate to their story.

The boyfriend explained that she was clinically diagnosed with depression and that this had been her fifth attempt to take her own life. The boyfriend was at work when it happened, and the girl's mom had found her, wrists cut and bleeding out all over the floor. The boyfriend had to rush to the hospital from work as his girlfriend was taken by ambulance. He then explained that the relationship between his girlfriend and her mom was fragile at best.

Once the girl started to calm down, and when there was complete silence, I turned my head toward the boyfriend, with my eyes closed, and asked, "How old are you?"

He replied, "I'm sixteen."

I then asked, "What do you do for work?"

He responded with, "I'm a carpenter, although I haven't been working much lately."

I began asking him more questions, which I won't share, but the fact was that this boy wasn't even an adult yet and he was living by himself, paying rent, working full-time, and having to deal with his girlfriend's suicidal tendencies on a frequent basis. I was amazed at his level of maturity.

Despite everything he had been through and was going through, he had a humble spirit and mindset about him, which challenged me. I wished them all the best and said that God loved them.

To this day, I have no idea what happened to them. Who knows, maybe one day I might find out. You never know who you will meet on any given day that will give you a renewed perspective. I couldn't see them, so I don't know what they look like, but God knows; and that's all that matters. My faith was challenged even more during my interaction with that young man.

The triage doctor finally came to see me. He had a very reassuring and confident tone, which was important for me because I couldn't see his eyes to know if he was telling me the truth. The eyes are the window to a person's soul. So, as you can imagine, it took me a lot longer to trust him. It didn't matter to me that he was a doctor; I had had bad experiences with trusting doctors before and knew firsthand what could happen when doctors were overly confident.

I had blood tests, and when they came back, the results showed that my kidneys were dehydrated and my white blood cell count was low. I was clearly fighting something off, and the doctor also suspected meningitis.

There are two types of meningitis. The first is type A—this is the kind of meningitis you definitely don't want to contract. Type A can lead to meningococcal meningitis—this is a serious disease that usually causes inflammation of the lining of the brain and the spinal cord, or blood poisoning, which can lead to the loss of limbs and even cause death. Type B, on the other hand, is only viral, and you can recover from that within two or three weeks of complete rest. However, you're still at a high risk of contracting type A if you don't follow the doctor's instructions of rest and medication.

The only way to be 100 percent certain if it is meningitis and whether you have type A or type B is to have a lumbar puncture. This is where the doctor gets a long needle and sticks it in your back, heading toward your spinal cord. Once he has reached your spinal cord, he then begins to drain your cerebrospinal fluid (fun fact: it looks like silver mercury, well at least mine did, and I've got a photo to prove it.) all while you are awake, and you feel everything!

However, I haven't told you the best part yet: According to the doctor treating me, there was only a 50 percent chance of success.

If the doctor fails to reach a specific point in your spine where he can drain the fluid, he can potentially cause damage to your spine. In other words, you could be paralyzed from the waist down, or in the worst case, even die. The doctor is literally flying blind, and he is only guided by the patient's voice telling him the moment when they feel a sharp pain all the way down their right leg—that's when the doctor's hit the right spot! (It's a rather interesting procedure, isn't it?) How's that for some comforting news for the doctor to hear...when the patient feels pain, the doctor's doing well!

Unfortunately for me, there was no other way around this, and it had to be done. Trust me, I asked if there was another way...many, many times.

The thought of not knowing if it would be a success or not worried me the most. I'm not someone who gambles at all, especially on his own life. I asked the doctor how many of these lumbar punctures he had performed, and he told me that he had only done one.

I asked him, "Was that one successful?"

And he replied, "Yes, it was. I assure you I know what I'm doing."

But that still didn't give me any confidence or peace at all.

I sat in that chair with my eyes closed and heard a still, small voice calmly say, "How did you end up here, Jarred?"

I answered sarcastically, "I don't know, why don't you tell me?"

The calm voice said, "Don't you trust me, Jarred?"

I instantly snapped back, "Of course, I do!"

The voice then simply answered with empathy, "Have faith in me, Jarred, just a little bit of faith."

This conversation went back and forth for over four hours. I kept on fighting the voice, who I believed was God. I knew he was right all along, but my egotistical, stubborn, and proud nature just wouldn't accept it.

The voice finally said to me, "Do you trust me?"

I replied, "Yes."

The voice was quiet, but I had a verse come to my heart and mind: *Be still and know that I am God.*

I turned to my mom and said, "Okay, I'm ready."

I was then taken to another room and prepared for the procedure. It was 12 a.m. and I laid on my left side, back facing toward the doctor. Before we began the procedure, Mom and I prayed that God would guide the doctor's hand and that the procedure was successful. I was petrified, but can you really blame me? My faith was being tested a lot during this whole experience.

The doctor got the first needle, which had just local anesthetic in it, and the local anesthetic only worked on a specific point in the muscle. After that, you felt everything!

I was lying there still like a statue, and I felt the long needle pass my outer muscle and into my inner muscle. It took some time before the doctor reached my spinal cord though. I wanted to see what was going on, so I asked Mom to film it for me. Sure enough, I felt every push and pull on my back, and it hurt a lot! Up until this point, I was quite accustomed to pain, but this was something else.

Suddenly, I feel this sharp stabbing pain right down the right side of my leg. I yelled out, "You got it!"

That's when the doctor began the extraction process of my spinal fluid.

I believe that God guided the doctor's hand to the exact spot he needed to be to extract my spinal fluid.

I was thankful that I listened to that still, small voice, and that eventually I had the faith needed to go through with this procedure because it wasn't easy. I have no idea what my life would have been like if the procedure had failed. I know that God would have taken care of me nonetheless, but as humans, we are experts at worrying. When we focus on the what-ifs in life, as I mentioned earlier, it takes away our ability to trust God and have faith in his ability to look after us.

If you are one of God's children, he won't ever give up on you. He loves and cares for you. There is this misconception that God is there with a hammer and the moment we fail at something, he hits us with that hammer. God is not like that at all, and it wasn't God's fault that I was in the hospital, either. God is merciful and knows what is best for our lives. He even said that his grace is sufficient for all our needs.

When we walk away from God, like a shepherd, be sure that he will bring you back to his fold. Failure is just another way God can redirect us back to him and build up our faith even more. When we return, it's usually on our knees in humility, asking for forgiveness.

God is always right, so stop fighting him.

After the procedure, I was taken directly up to a ward. Mom left to get some sleep, which she deserved. I can't thank my parents enough, especially my mom, who was going through her own health issues with her heart at the time. She even had a halter monitor on her heart reading for high levels of stress. This situation was definitely the perfect time to test for stress.

The first night in the hospital wasn't pleasant at all. My head was throbbing like a jackhammer breaking up concrete. I was still unable to see, and it was just me alone with my thoughts.

The next morning, the doctor who had done my lumbar puncture came in to see me, but I still couldn't see him. He told me the results had come back confirming that it was type B meningitis; however, I wasn't out of danger yet. I was still at risk of contracting type A if I wasn't careful and didn't rest. I didn't like hearing the fact that I needed to rest, because rest didn't, and still doesn't, mesh well with my brain.

Up until this point, I was going at full speed, and I gave life 110 percent every second of every day. So it was clear that my body was telling me to rest, but I never listened to anyone.

However, I listened to God, and I believed that he showed me that I needed to rest.

God has a funny way of getting us to listen, doesn't he?

It took me three weeks to fully recover. I spent the first week at home in bed mostly sleeping. The other two weeks I spent trying to rest, but my version of rest was lightly running and doing body-weight workouts. You would think that after a big health scare, I'd have learned my lesson by now?

In my opinion, failing to take care of your body is one of the worst failures. When you don't have your health, you have nothing. That is why it's important that we look after ourselves. It takes time, but after a while, you finally realize one of the best lessons you can learn in life: Faithful humility.

Humility is not feeling low about yourself or having thoughts of self-pity, wishing that things would be different if you had another chance. In humility, there is strong and sound wisdom. Proverbs says it best: God resists the proud, but he gives grace to the humble. Pride stops our faith in God, and instead we put faith in ourselves. If you can learn one thing from this chapter, it's this: God is real, he loves you, and don't be like me; surrender your pride daily to God because there is nothing worse than relying on yourself more than God.

When we have faith the size of only a mustard seed, will we then be able to experience God do some great things, beyond our wildest imaginations.

CHAPTER 9
God-Given Purpose

Purpose Isn't the Destination; It's an Ever-Changing, Exciting Part of Our Journey

I've had a great deal of conversations on *The Story Box* about *purpose*. It's one of my favorite topics to speak with people about. Purpose is a massive—and I mean massive—part of a person's life. People almost feel like if they don't have a purpose, they aren't worth anything. Well, I'm here to tell you that just because you might not know what your purpose is right now, it doesn't make you any less of a human being! In fact, I think that it's time to change the thought process around purpose, don't you?

Firstly, I want to say that you are worthy of love, happiness, joy, peace, abundance, and fulfillment in your life.

Now, I'd like those that struggle to know their worth to say:

"I am worth it."

"I am valuable."

"I do deserve love, peace, joy, and abundance."

Say it until you start believing it! Because once you start believing that you are worth it, that is going to help with finding your purpose in life. How? Half the battle for many people is believing the lie that *they aren't worth anything and they don't have a purpose.*

I was sitting in a sales training meeting one afternoon to help improve our team's house-selling performance. At this point in my life, I thought my purpose was to sell houses for a living. My boss always expected more from us, and I think he expected a lot more from me. I had far more responsibilities than any other team member, and I also needed to keep up with my weekly targets that my boss had set.

The sales training manager, who was also a successful real estate agent, went through how we were meant to speak with buyers over the phone to either get a listing or a sale. He said that we should always keep it to a two-minute limit. Anything over that was wasting our precious time.

However, I had *conversations* with people over the phone, and more often than not, the buyers appreciated that about me and I got good results.

We ran through a scenario with the sales training manager listening in. I made the first call and spoke with the person for over five minutes.

When I got off the phone, the sales manager said, "Jay, you like to repeat information a lot to the buyers, don't you?"

I looked at him and replied, "Yes, because more often than not, people forget half of the things you say to them within the first few seconds. I like to repeat what I say so people can remember. I get better results that way."

The manager just said, "You like to triple qualify buyers."

When I began to explain the importance of repetition to him, he didn't seem too interested.

If I repeat things in this book, it's because I want you to understand its significance and importance so that you're able to remember it. There has been a lot in this book so far already to take in and there will be more to come.

But what I have learned is that *persistent repetition of good things is another key to living a successful life*—a life filled with purposeful happiness. The more you tell yourself that you are worth it, the more you begin to believe it.

This is the first step to knowing one's purpose in life.

Secondly, God designed life with purpose already; nothing that God created is without a purpose, and that includes you. Just living is the best purpose of all. God said that he knew you before you were even born! That tells me that if you are alive today, you weren't born to be stuck; you were born to thrive. You were designed with unique qualities unlike those of anyone else in this world. That, my friend, is purpose.

I *Am* versus I *Do*

For many years, I believed that it was my purpose and destiny to become a famous Hollywood filmmaker like my idol Steven Spielberg. People even said to me that I was going to be "the next Spielberg." When people asked, "So what do you do for work, Jarred?" I immediately replied, "I am a filmmaker." It became like second nature to me—each time someone asked me that question, I always put "I am" in front.

To better understand your purpose, you need to look at *who you are* versus *what you do.* Quite often, people get these confused, and that's when they believe that their purpose lies with what they do instead of who they are. I know this because this was exactly my belief for many years!

Who you are is reflected by your character, values, beliefs, and morals. This is what you will carry into a job and not the other way around. You don't need a job to feel worth something in society. You should have a job, though, because it is good to work and contribute to your economy. But don't get fooled by the trap society has plagued many with: if you don't have a great income, a nice car, big house, beautiful wife or husband, a family, or even a fun job, you aren't successfully living a purpose-filled life. And therefore, that makes you worthless to people who may seem like they have it all. You never know what's really happening on the inside.

Don't get me wrong: for those that do have all these nice things, it's not bad. I know many millionaires, even some billionaires, who have everything that money could ever buy. But some have said to me, "Jarred, what is great wealth without a fulfilling purpose behind you? It's just great wealth, isn't it? It won't ever fulfill you long-term. When you live a life serving others while using that great wealth—now that is a wealthy purpose not to be taken for granted."

I once sat down with a good friend for a conversation around purpose and what it means to not only find it but live it out. He said, "Jay, your purpose isn't the destination; it's only part of the journey." And he was right.

This was exactly where I got stuck for many years, thinking that the moment I found my purpose (in film), I'd be happy, wealthy, and fulfilled.

I think that society has conditioned us to believe that purpose is found in what we do rather than who we are. And so many people chase it, like I did.

The moment we get the job of our dreams, our purpose—according to society—is suddenly found. That didn't happen for me, though. I thought filmmaking was my purpose, but as I was living it, I felt like there was still something missing—something deeper, more profound and enriching to my life than just a job I had wanted since I was eight years old.

I needed to start asking myself all the tough questions I had chosen to avoid. Because, after all, I had found my purpose, right?

What would you do if everything you had—and yes, I mean *everything*—was taken away from you? All that you had left were the clothes on your back. Who would you be then?

There is a profound story in the Bible from the book of Job about how God allowed Satan to take everything away from Job's life. Satan believed that Job would curse God after everything was stripped away from him. Now, Job was a righteous man—a man who feared God and worshipped him daily. Job was also a rich man because God had blessed his faithfulness. In one day, Job lost his family, his riches, his house, and even his health. His wife even told him to curse God and die.

However, Job got down on his knees and said, "God giveth and God taketh, blessed be the name of the Lord."

Those beautiful words inspire me every time I read or hear them.

Job understood that his purpose wasn't in earthly things at all—it was in his character, integrity, and how he worshipped God. That should be your purpose too.

Everything that I am right now is because of God. I know that he has put me on this Earth to serve him and do great things in his name. I may not know what they are yet, but he has given me small insights into working toward fulfilling his calling for my life.

There's a special song written by Ron Hamilton that fits perfectly in line with the purpose God has given me. It's called "Rejoice in The Lord." It talks about how God never moves without having a reason.

Here is what I've been guilty of on my path to finding purpose. The moment something bad happened in my life, I immediately started blaming God. It was all his fault. If he knows what's good for me, then why am I stuck in this dark hole?

It's never God's fault at all. His purpose for your life is always perfect because he made you! Remember, God will give you exactly what you need, and when you need it. It might not always be what you want, but it's always what we need. Finding our purpose with God becomes easier when we trust in his perfect plan and have faith the size of a mustard seed. It's that easy! Don't make it hard for yourself.

The song also talks about how God doesn't make mistakes and always knows the outcomes of our actions.

I have gone through so many trying times on the way to knowing my purpose. God knew well before I did that I'd be on the path of an eagle. And when I was knocked down and in my lowest possible moments, God didn't make a mistake. He enabled me to get back up and continue to soar. He tested the strength of my faith in his perfect plan so I could start seeing his purpose for my life clearer.

When you go through horrible times, remember that if you believe in God, then what you are going through is a trying process to refine you into pure gold, fit for your God-given purpose. God will build your purpose through challenges, failures, and moments of pain and struggle. If we all had the same attitude as Job—"Lord, what are you trying to teach me here?"—life might be more peaceful for us.

One of my favorite parts of the song is when Ron Hamilton sheds light on the fact that God will strengthen his children, and in his love, he will purge us of anything unclean. Because of that, I know for a fact that my heavenly father knows what's best for my future, and I trust that he will always take care of me.

You might be reading this and believe differently, and that is fine, but just know this: there is no better purpose than a

God-given purpose, and you are worthy not because I said so, but because God said and made you so. He made your worth more than gold itself. Gold is his pavement, and you weren't made to be just pavement. You were made by God to soar above the heavens.

It's time for you to start believing that.

CHAPTER 10

The Story Box

Be Persistent to Remain Consistent at the Things You Want

Back in early 2018, I had this wild and crazy idea to start a podcast. The original idea was centered around sitting down with my friend Amos Fernandez and watching films with good stories, so that we could do a short review about the film and then try to get more people to watch that film. If the film was great and if we rated it over four stars, it went into a virtual box I called, "The Story Box." We only reached five episodes in total, but our numbers for a podcast just starting out were quite decent considering we weren't very consistent.

It wasn't long before the podcast just went dead, and it became clear to me that it was rather taxing in both finances and time. I also didn't have a great vision or mission for it to begin with, and I had no idea how much work it would be. Truth be told, I wasn't ready for this big commitment. I deleted everything online that concerned *The Story Box* and went about my life.

What I learned from starting my first podcast was that if you're going to do something, do it well the first time, but also never be afraid to just have a go! If your idea doesn't work out in the end, that is still okay. I have had many failed business ideas, and I even failed at both my film businesses—the one thing I thought I was going to be great at.

Back then, *The Story Box* was a golden nugget that needed to fail in order for me to realize its true potential later on. Rome wasn't built in a day; great ideas take time to nurture and grow. Be patient and enjoy the process along the way, and if you fail, enjoy that failure, pick yourself up, and try again.

Like I have mentioned many times in this book: it's through our failures that we learn one of life's most valuable and greatest lessons: *humility.* We aren't better than anyone else; we all breathe the same air; we all have minds; we all have blood running through our veins. What makes you better than another person? Nothing—we are all equal in the eyes of God.

The Story Box just sat there in my mind for over a year. I had no desire to continue it, and I made a promise to myself that if I was going to start it again, I needed to be 100 percent committed to it. And I certainly wouldn't leave it five episodes in again; the vision and mission needed to be clear to me as well; otherwise, I wouldn't commit to it.

During the fourth month into my real estate job, a friend reached out to me and asked if I was considering starting up *The Story Box* podcast again, as he had been a fan from the beginning. This was a life-changing question because I replied, "I'll have a think about it." And eventually, I did!

Around August of 2019, I wasn't feeling happy or fulfilled at my job. Certain events transpired at my workplace that signified it was time for me to leave. So, I started the grueling process of looking for another job while I was still working for my current boss. Several initial opportunities seemed to spring up, and they all looked rather enticing. Come September, I had just about had enough of what was going on in my job, so I made the decision to resign without having a new job lined up.

My resignation came as a shock to pretty much everyone: my boss, his wife, my sales manager, and everyone in the office. I even had two people who were highly influential in the company try and get me to stay. Before I even considered revoking my resignation letter, I told them how I was feeling and what I wanted changed—and mind you, it wasn't for my benefit, either; it was to further improve the team.

When I resigned on Friday, I said that my final day would be Sunday. However, I ended up going into work on Monday and Tuesday to help with trying to sell two properties, as I didn't want any of my buyers to miss out. I had formed close enough relationships with each of them that leaving abruptly would have been rude. I valued my character and integrity above anything else in that job, and I'd be damned if I stopped valuing it for the sake of leaving the job.

I then set a meeting with my sales manager, my boss, and his wife for Tuesday afternoon. My sales manager arrived, and he called me into the meeting with him. However, my boss and his wife didn't show. I accepted their decision to not show up, and my sales manager explained it was better for them to just cut all ties. He also explained that they had accepted my resignation and they couldn't change the way their business was structured, not even for me. I said that it would have been nice if they had told me this themselves.

Strangely, when my sales manager told me they had accepted my letter of resignation, I got this massive tingle all the way down my entire body. But I felt calm and at peace. My sales manager thanked me and said that he could see I was going to go far.

This company has this lowering ritual that when an employee leaves a team, there is this "intimidation" walk out. But, as I gathered my things and said goodbye to one of the assistants, I held my head high as I walked out of that place because I had kept my character and integrity intact the whole time. I didn't move when the waves kept beating down on me and held true to what I believed was right. I might not have had a job, but I had something far more valuable in my possession.

Young people, listen to me, please.

Don't ever, not even for a second, trade your character or integrity for anything! It doesn't matter if you are threatened, scared, or want to give in. *Hold fast and stand true!* I believe that God still protected me during that whole situation, even when I walked away from him for that whole year.

I drove home and turned on the radio. The song that came on was the same song that had "saved" me in a way when I tried to end my life months earlier. However, it had a different meaning behind it this time. Even though I no longer had a job or any idea of where to go next, I was at peace and knew that leaving was the best decision.

For that whole year, I had been on a journey of self-discovery. The loss of my dog Joy, the breakup with the woman who I thought I'd be with for the rest of my life, all the failures and abuse I endured—it all made me start asking myself the tougher questions.

What do I really want to do?

Who am I really?

What is my purpose in life?

And why suddenly now?

I continued the process of looking for a new job. While that was happening, I also started planning to bring *The Story Box* podcast back. My business partner at the time wanted to be part of the podcast as a cohost, and I said that was fine. (Oh, I didn't mention that while I was working in real estate, I also tried to get my film career back off the ground, but with a business partner this time around.) However, I'm a man of action: if I truly want something, I'll go after it and work incredibly hard to get it. However, he was the total opposite; he liked to take his time. And often, he hardly got anything done.

So, I reached out to a few of my friends who had interesting stories to share, and they were all kind enough to say yes and give me a chance. I then told my business partner that I had started the difficult process of reaching out and organizing guests.

He didn't take kindly to me doing that and his exact words were: "I feel like the train has left with you on it, and I've been left back at the station."

I couldn't believe it. We had been talking about doing this for weeks, if not months, up until this point, and we had just kept putting it off. Now that I had taken the first step in building *The Story Box*, my business partner wasn't happy about it.

We therefore decided that it was best for us to take a break, since I had already started *The Story Box*, and I had made the decision then to go and study teaching at a university. (I did end up going to a university for one semester, but that is another story for another time.) However, I was very undecided again with where I wanted to go in life. And can you really blame me? I was lost and needed to find the right direction. The only thing that I really knew that made sense to me at that time was doing *The Story Box* again.

Looking back now, I understand how he must have felt, but it was still his choice to leave. I respected his decision and wished him all the best. I then messaged him from time to time to see how he was, but he never replied. This whole situation is just another example of God protecting me and guiding me toward the right path—the path that an eagle should take is soaring high in the skies, not down on the ground.

The split from my business partner happened around the end of September. By this point, I had already been to several job interviews, all of which seemed rather enticing (even though I had decided to go to college and study, mind you). I went to two interviews for another real estate company, and six interviews for various recruitment companies, which were all spread across Sydney. If I was going to go to college, I still needed a job.

One recruitment company stood out from the rest. I received a phone call from the hiring manager, and she sounded extremely nice. After she finished asking me a great deal of questions, she invited me to a group interview.

I had been to only one group interview before, and it sucked! You're literally trying to compete with everyone else for one position in the company, but instead of one-on-one interviews in which you don't see other candidates, you see everyone you are competing with. I find that experience to be rather unnerving, which I believe is why they do it. This company was only looking for the best, the stand-out performer.

I arrived at the interview wearing my nice blue suit as I'd do for any job interview. I even wore a suit at a job interview with Apple, and needless to say, I didn't get that job. But no other candidate at this interview was wearing a full suit (to my shock); they were all in "smart casual." There was a total of six of us, and as we introduced ourselves, it was clear that everyone else was much older than me and far more experienced. I felt like a fish not fit for the ocean but for a fish tank.

We were split up into small groups for a sales presentation that we were to perform later. We were told that the CEO of the whole company would be watching the presentations. We were given one item to try and sell. And while I had done a simílar scenario in my Apple interview, I was still nervous—I like to be behind the camera directing talent, not being the talent. Believe it or not, I'm an introvert and a shy person.

We went through the normal routine of job interviews: learning about the company, the position we were interviewing for, what the job entailed, benefits, and so forth. We even went for a tour of the different departments. You know, all the standard stuff, but it really was quite an enticing place to work. The perks were excellent, but I didn't feel at peace there. However, I was still curious and kept going along with it.

The fun part of the interview finally arrived where each group had five minutes to come up with a sales pitch where all three of us in the group had to say something about the item we had chosen to sell. The presentation, in my opinion, seemed to go well.

We were then told to wait for a few minutes, and then suddenly, the lady told us that there had been a slight change in plans. The original plan was that we were going to have to come back on another day for the CEO's ten-minute speed interviews. However, they decided to have the interviews right then.

I put up my hand to go first, mainly because I wanted to go home quicker. I walked into the board room and sat down opposite the CEO. I had a copy of my resume, so I handed that to him.

He looked at me and said, "Great job with your sales pitch."

I replied with a simple, "Thank you."

He then looked over my resume, nodded his head a few times, and asked, "Jarred, why do you want to work here?"

I didn't really have to think too hard about that question because my answer was, "I want to help people. I was helping people get a house while in real estate, and I thought why not use that same skill set, but this time help people get a job."

The CEO seemed to like that truthful answer; he could clearly see something in me that I couldn't see then. I answered all his questions within the ten minutes. We finished the interview, I shook his hand goodbye, and then I said my goodbyes to everyone that I had interviewed with.

On the train ride home, I thought about the whole interview, and for some reason I kept thinking about that one question the CEO asked me: why did I want to work there? I answered him truthfully, so why couldn't I get it out of my mind?

I then realized something important; it was like another light bulb went off in my head.

Here is what I figured out.

Yes, I could get a job working for this massive company, climb the corporate ladder, and do a damn fine job at it too. But I knew that I wouldn't be happy. Yes, I could help someone find a job and that would be satisfying on several levels, but if that was all I was there for, then the job wasn't for me.

I was looking at my future all wrong—I was chasing security with money because I had bills to pay and responsibilities to look after.

But like God had said to me way back in 2018, when I was fighting him about where I was at in life—did I really trust him?

All I knew at that time was that I had to turn to him for answers.

So, when I got home that day, I went into my room and knelt beside my bed. There is something about being in that submissive position that God honors and respects. Like I have mentioned, I had walked away from God that whole year, and I blamed him for all the pain I had experienced.

I realized though on that train ride home that it wasn't God's fault at all, and I had just been running from the pain instead of facing it. I asked God to forgive me, and I made the commitment to never walk away from God ever again, no matter what happened. I was going to trust him to take care of me, even though I didn't have a job and my money was running dangerously low.

The next day while on my run, I had another light-bulb moment—this time it was exactly what *The Story Box* podcast was going to become. God gave me the vision and mission all in that moment. He showed me that stories have incredible power to move nations, to change hearts and lives for either good or bad. Stories have always been the backbone of our humanity, and hardly anyone gets to hear the real stories.

The Story Box exists today because I want to help people understand their worth and realize their true potential. This, I believe, is ultimately my God-given purpose. I do this by unboxing the stories of men and women from every field imaginable, and from all over the world.

As of December 2021, *The Story Box* has grown to reach over 160 countries and over twenty-eight million people. I have personally unboxed the stories of over seven hundred individuals, some of them extremely high-profile people. I never thought that would be possible in the first year. God has blessed and taken care of me during a wild global pandemic, and he used that pandemic to help grow *The Story Box* to newfound heights.

Just think that if I had taken the recruitment position, I probably would have been out of a job. And this book wouldn't be in your hands today.

People have asked me what it takes to run a successful podcast and I say, "It's not about whether *The Story Box* is successful or not—to me it's about how many more lives can be changed for the better. How many more individuals can be inspired, motivated, challenged, and even educated by others' stories. I'm not ever going to stop until God tells me to. But until then, I will continue working as hard as possible to help people realize their worth."

What many people don't understand about starting a podcast is that it's a big commitment. Not just financially, but you're investing time, energy, and resources into it, as well as a great deal of emotional and mental power. It can be rather taxing, and there have been moments when I've needed to take one or even two days to just refocus and reenergize myself. You may not realize it, but speaking with people is hard work, especially in an interview-style setting.

Back in October of 2019, I reached out to someone who was high profile within the real estate sector—Mat Steinwede. When I contacted him via Instagram, I didn't even think he'd see my message, but he did. He responded almost immediately, and he was keen to be a guest. I couldn't believe it—my first high-profile guest for *The Story Box*.

We arranged a time and date, and when the day came, I was both excited and nervous. I couldn't believe that I was meeting a top performer in his field. I got in my car and began driving the nearly two-hour trip to where we had set the meeting. Upon my arrival, I walked into the office and waited several minutes before Mat's assistant came out and introduced herself to me. She then began to apologize about the fact Mat wasn't in the office and that he was back in Sydney in a meeting. It was right in that very moment that I realized something important. If I wanted to do this podcast and do it well, I needed to do whatever it took to get this meeting with Mat.

Mat's assistant gave me his number and told me to call him now to arrange another meeting time and place. And with my shaky tone of voice, I called Mat. We arranged to meet at 12:30 p.m. near the big water fountain at Hyde Park. (It was 11:30 when I called him.) I ended the call with Mat, said my goodbyes and thanked his assistant, got in my car, and away I went back down to Sydney.

When I finally found parking, which is notoriously difficult and pricy to find in the Sydney central business district, I was already running five minutes late. And then I had to try and find the fountain at Hyde Park and I desperately needed to use the toilet. Yes, I know…I had lived in Sydney for over twenty-three years and I still didn't know where the fountain was! Thank God there was some running event on, so I stopped one of the older runners and asked for directions to the toilets first and then the fountain. (I put that old stereotype of men not wanting to ask for directions to shame that day.)

It's not that hard to spot Mat Steinwede; he's a mountain of a man—tall with muscles on muscles, and he's always got a videographer with him. I was wearing my sarcastic "Harvard, Just Kidding" shirt that day with my old Nike shorts with a hole in the back pocket. I was sweating when I walked up to Mat. I know, great first impression of me! Late, not wearing the best of clothes, and I was sweating!

But Mat was so calm, collected, present, understanding, and kind, which made me feel at ease while doing the interview. Since this was literally my first "big-time" interview with someone semi famous, I prepared a long list of questions, which Mat answered well within ten minutes of the interview. I was hoping to get more from him, and so for the next fourteen minutes, I asked him some questions from the top of my head. It was rather daunting at first, but eventually the interview concluded. Mat and I took a photo together, and then I went back to my car.

During the drive home, I kept thinking about Mat's story from homeless to becoming the number-one real estate agent for McGrath at that time in Australia. My emotions were still buzzing with excitement—it was then that I realized that this was exactly what I needed to be doing for the rest of my life (or at least until God told me otherwise). And I was going to do whatever it took to build *The Story Box* to reach every single person on this planet with a story. (Ambitious...I know! But I believe doable.)

Lockdown

In December 2019, the world was told of an illness called coronavirus. It spread across the world so quickly that world health leaders didn't know how to contain it. Boarders to countries remained open long enough for infectious people to enter countries and spread the virus around, causing mass infections, including here in Australia.

COVID-19, as it started becoming known, spread to greater parts of Australia, including Sydney, where I live. The minister for health and our premier decided to introduce the first line of restrictions: you weren't allowed to travel unless it was essential, and most cafés and restaurants had to close their doors or just try to survive by doing takeout; gyms, pubs, and clubs were also closed. Any parks and outdoor workout equipment were barred and banned—you could only walk or run. You were not allowed to sit on any park benches, and there was a limit of people allowed in houses at any one time.

We had to practice a term now infamous in the history books: "social distancing." Places of worship were now online, and weddings could only have ten people maximum, all practicing social distancing and wearing masks. The same went for funerals.

I had never experienced anything like this before, and neither had anyone else.

When I first started doing interviews for *The Story Box*, I traveled around and met the guests in person. I preferred that style, and I felt more comfortable doing it that way. When the lockdown restrictions happened, and I couldn't travel for interviews, I was worried about what would happen to my podcast.

It wasn't long after lockdown began that everyone started doing meetings through a program called Zoom. Zoom was honestly a lifesaver; it enabled conference-style high-quality recording for free! When you face a challenge like COVID, you pivot and improvise—you do your best to make it work.

Zoom meetings became a thing, and before I knew it, I was doing more and more Zoom-based podcast interviews with people from all over the world. And I found that people now had more time to be interviewed.

But also, many other people had decided to launch their own podcasts. In the space of a few months, over a million new podcasts had been introduced into the already flooded market. And where was *The Story Box*? Still trying to climb to the top from way down at the bottom.

During lockdown, I had nothing but time on my hands to figure out how I was going to build *The Story Box* and still work toward my vision. At first, none of the higher-profile people were giving me a chance. I didn't know the first thing about sending out invitations via email. I received countless rejection replies, and I couldn't understand why. I thought I had a great idea. However, it just so happened that because of COVID, yes, high-profile people were more accessible, but they were being pitched by hundreds of other podcasters.

When I started *The Story Box*, I knew that I was going to face some form of rejection. I just had no idea the sheer amount of it. I was receiving thirty to fifty rejection emails a day. I'd get maybe one or three people that said yes, which made me thrilled that someone said yes to me. In 2020 alone, I sent out well over four thousand, maybe over five thousand, emails to a wide range of people. Guess how many said yes to me?

Well…four hundred, or thereabout.

And for those four hundred people that did give me a chance, I'll forever be grateful for them believing in me and what I was trying to do with the podcast.

I spoke on a Mindvalley podcast called *SuperHumans at Work* (it's now no longer a part of Mindvalley) to a live audience of about 270 people on Zoom. I had never done anything like this before, and at first, I was nervous. But as the conversation got rolling, so did I. The topic of conversation was on how to overcome rejection. One of the things I said during the conversation was, "Rejection is a way to help you move forward and enhance your resilience because rejection is never going away. You just have to learn to appreciate it."

The Story Box wouldn't be where it is today without the rejection. The rejection never defined who I was as a person, but it certainly did grow my mindset.

Because the conversations on most other podcasts were about COVID-19, I decided to ask questions not related to COVID. Instead, I asked my guests questions about their interesting lives to give the listeners more inspiring stories. I think the guests not only appreciated this, but my growing audience did as well.

I also started to realize the importance of courageous vulnerability and sharing some of my own stories with not only the guests, but my audience. What you saw and heard on *The Story Box* is who I am in real life. For me there are no gray areas. I strive to live in full integrity and be my true authentic self, quirks and all. Because of this, my guests felt comfortable with sharing some of their deep and personal stories. And it also made my audience feel more connected to me as the host and to the guests too.

Joel McHale

It was June 2020, and I had been receiving countless rejection emails from people I had reached out to. But I decided to do something even more bold and reach out to Hollywood celebrities. At this stage, I barely had the kind of reach or numbers that I do now—I still gave it a go, though. I had expected that everyone was going to say no to me, but my grandy's words kept coming back to me: *if you don't ask, you don't get.* I kept wishing that Grandy was still alive so he could give me advice with overcoming rejection.

It was a Sunday afternoon, and I spent over four hours researching and collecting data on who I was going to reach out to next. I had over five hundred emails drafted and ready to send on Monday to various publicists, agents, and managers of some of Hollywood's biggest stars. I sent every email individually that Sunday night and waited for the bombardment of rejection replies to come my way.

Sure enough, two days later, I got one, two, three, four... fifty rejections. Some were nice and took the time to respond to me individually, while others just wrote a few words: "Hi, Jay. Not available, sorry."

I always responded back and asked when the best time was to reach out again. However, hardly anyone replied. A couple of lovely people responded a second time, and I can't thank those wonderful people enough for their kindness.

It was Friday morning, and up until that point I had received about two hundred rejections, or "not-now emails" as I call them. I got back from my run and checked my email to see in the body of one: "We can definitely make this happen."

I couldn't believe it, and when I checked who it was, I was even more astonished. Joel McHale is one of Hollywood's most respected and well-known names, and he said yes to being a guest on my podcast! I instantly replied and organized a time and date with Joel's publicist.

At that stage of *The Story Box*, Joel McHale was the only one out of the two hundred replies that said yes. But…it only takes one yes to start a chain reaction. Joel even said to me at the end of our conversation, "I hope this gets you one more person."

You only need one person to believe in what you are doing in order to help grow your vision. No one, and I mean no one, knew who Jay Fantom was when I first started my podcast. If I didn't reach out and ask, and if I had of given up when all the rejection emails came, *The Story Box* wouldn't be where it is today. Persistence and asking for what you want *does* work.

So, pick yourself back up. It's time for you to get back in the air, my friend, and start soaring higher this time because now you are stronger than you were before.

Matthew McConaughey

I went from interviewing friends to interviewing the legendary Academy Award-winning actor Matthew McConaughey. How did this happen? Well, it's quite the story.

One of the Hollywood celebrities I wanted to talk to was Matthew McConaughey. And when I reached out to Matthew's people, I thought there was no way that he would want to be on my show. This was around August 2020.

The Story Box hadn't really grown to the extent of other big shows like Joe Rogan's, Lewis Howes's, or even Russell Brand's. However, on the seventeenth of August, I received an email that shocked the life out of me!

The email said that Matthew was launching his new book in October and to touch base with his publicity team again then. I mean, I was literally over the moon, because that email gave me hope that there was a chance that I might get to speak with Matthew McConaughey in October.

October came around and it couldn't have come sooner. So, at the beginning of October, I sent a follow-up email. And sure enough, I got another reply—but it wasn't the one I had been expecting. Here I was thinking that I'd be able to speak with Matthew in October. However, that wasn't the case.

I understood that because *The Story Box* wasn't at the level of the top-industry leaders, it was a big ask for Matthew to give up his time for an interview on my show. I was placed way, way, way down the long list of possible shows to appear on. There was no real guarantee either that I would get time with Matthew. But I didn't give up. A chance is still a chance.

The email said for me to wait until November. So that's exactly what I did, and I once again reached out to Matthew's publicity team.

But when November came, again I received an email to tell me to wait until December.

However, this time they asked if I was interested in speaking with another one of Hollywood's great actors: Boris Kodjoe. I instantly jumped at the opportunity, and I ended up having a great conversation with Boris.

Finally, December rolled around and I was keen to see if an interview with Matthew was possible before the end of the year. Sadly, my hopes faded when they told me that I had to wait until January.

Still, it was a chance—a chance that I took and believed in.

It was December 16th, and I decided to touch base with Matthew's publicity team one last time before the end of the year, just to see if we were able to book in a time and date. I didn't hear anything back for two days, and I thought I had probably annoyed the living daylights out of them.

But then it happened. The moment I had been persistently waiting patiently for...

I was doing some work when I heard my phone buzz. It was an email from Matthew's publicity team, which said, "Jay, how does January 8th look for you at 11 a.m. PST and 1 p.m. CT?"

That was all I needed to see. I leaped at the opportunity. I didn't care what time of the morning or what else I had on that day; I'd make myself available for the whole day if I had to. I replied confirming the time and sent over a link for Matthew to join on the day. That was the best way to end an already great year for *The Story Box*.

So, I decided to buy Matthew's new book *Greenlights* just to prepare for our interview. I read the book in two days; I loved it that much! There aren't many books that I can complete in that space of time, but Matthew's book had me hooked. I even went back over the book several times, making notes in the pages, just so I didn't forget important points. I then listened to every single episode of all the podcasts Matthew had done, making notes. I wanted to make sure that the questions I asked were completely different from the ones that were asked by other podcast hosts. I wanted to "unbox" things that Matthew hadn't shared before.

Eventually, I came up with a few good questions that I wanted to ask Matthew. I had two set questions that I asked every single guest on my show, and I was extremely curious about what Matthew's answers would be to them. (Go and listen to the episode to find out his responses to those two questions; search *The Story Box* on either YouTube or any other podcast platform.)

The day of the interview came around fast. It was scheduled for 6 a.m. Australian time. I was up at 3 a.m., buzzing with delight and nervous energy. I went for a run at around

3:45 a.m., to clear my head. I got home at around 5:45 a.m. with fifteen minutes to get myself organized.

Finally, it was time!

However, I got an email to say that Matthew had joined another Zoom link for a meeting I had scheduled in March 2021. I thought, *oh crap, crap, crap*—I must have sent him the wrong link by accident. I quickly emailed the right link attached and an apology. Here I was wasting the precious time of one of Hollywood's greatest stars, and I felt like such an amateur. And, of course, all the what-ifs attacked my brain, the worst one being: What if he gets fed up with this amateur Aussie and just decides to cancel it?

I then received another email notification saying that Matthew had tried joining the same link as he did before again. This time, I quickly started that Zoom meeting room, and thankfully I was able to let Matthew in! My heart was racing—this was the one interview that I didn't want to mess up. When Matthew and I connected, I quickly said that I was sorry.

His response was, "The 17th of March, 2021, or something like that? Wait a minute, I'm not that early."

That calmed me down, and he said it while laughing, and while he was about to take a sip of his coffee. (Don't quote me on the coffee part. Could have been water in a coffee mug.)

The meeting with Matthew was only scheduled for thirty minutes, and I had already wasted ten of those precious thirty minutes. Yet when Matthew and I started talking, there was this flow of conversation. Those thirty minutes turned into almost one hour, and I could have gone a lot longer, but I had another meeting scheduled.

Now why would I end a conversation with Matthew McConaughey early? Well, I also wanted to be respectful of his valuable time. I think he appreciated this, and he said to me at the end, "You are welcome. I could do it all day. I look forward to our next time." I was on cloud nine for the rest of the day.

I immediately sent an email to Matthew's publicity team and thanked them for their kindness and patience with my persistent nature. They responded back with, "Matthew really enjoyed the conversation." They even extended the kindness further when they included Matthew's media team's details to help with the promotion of his episode. It went crazy after Matthew shared it.

Don't give up trying.

An eagle is persistent because it knows it will forever remain consistent at the things it wants. That is all part of being on the path of an eagle.

Tony Robbins

Way back when I first started *The Story Box*, I created a "wish list"—names of people who I wanted to interview and whose stories I wanted to share.

The first name on my list was, of course, Steven Spielberg. The second name was none other than Tony Robbins—the number one life coach, philanthropist, and business strategist.

It was during 2020 that I began to reach out to Tony Robbins. And in October, I finally received an email from someone who worked closely with Tony's team. We organized an initial meeting to talk and go over some details, which for someone like Tony is a standard procedure and one that I have become rather accustomed to.

We set the meeting for October 15th. However, I then received an email saying that there was a conflict with that person's schedule and that they would send questions via email instead. I felt a little crushed inside because I had received those emails in the past, and I never heard back from them again no matter how many emails I sent to follow up.

I didn't give up, though, and I came up with an idea that I thought might work. When in doubt, take a creative risk.

I created a short video explaining why I wanted to speak with Tony, what my podcast was about, how it got started, who my audience at the time was, and where I envisioned it going. I also sent three interviews from guests that I had had great conversations with. These guests were even "associated" with Tony in some way, so I thought it was good to let him see how I interviewed them.

The email seemed to work because a day after I sent it, I got a reply. Although they still couldn't organize a time for me with Tony (whose time is rather limited), they did have some other high-profile people that were interested in sharing their stories. I instantly jumped at the opportunity, and through this incredible chance, I was able to speak with Peter Mallouk, the *New York Times* bestselling author of *The Path* and *Unshakeable*, which he wrote *with* Tony Robbins. I also spoke with Ally Brooke, a former member of the popular girl band Fifth Harmony.

Fast-forward to January 2021. I sent my Matthew McConaughey interview to Tony's contact and again asked if it was possible to speak with Tony. I received a reply within a day saying that Tony was doing select media interviews on a particular date and if I was free that day, to send in a time that was good for me.

I literally dropped to my knees in utter disbelief and sheer gratitude. This was something I had worked incredibly hard for all year, and it was finally happening. In that moment of realization, I just couldn't seem to get my head around the fact that I was going to be able to tick Tony's name off my wish list!

The interview was scheduled for a week after I received the email confirmation, and for some reason, I kept thinking that something would happen a day before this interview, so I guess I began preparing myself to receive the worst news.

However, there wasn't any.

When the day of the interview arrived, I was so nervous that I extended my morning run just to burn off a bit of that energy. It seemed to calm and focus me, and when I got home, I did some preliminary tests, checks, and read over my questions, and information. Then the moment arrived.

Tony Robbins entered the Zoom meeting and immediately we began to jell. His energy was infectious, and I bounced off it. This settled my nerves even more. I took a deep breath in and out, said a quick prayer, and away the interview went.

The conversation flowed well, and we spoke on a deeper level when Tony shared stories from his childhood that shaped his attitude and values today.

I really didn't want the conversation to end, as I felt like I could have spoken with Tony for hours and not get tired. Then came my small moment to share with Tony my CAP method. I also shared my favorite quote, "Be persistent to remain consistent at the things you want."

Tony agreed with what I expressed, and he then began to tell me that he respected me and could tell that I was a high achiever. I was practically bursting with joy—I mean, I know Tony is just a man, but this was a remarkable honor.

And trust me, it gets better...

Going into my conversation with Tony, I had a small goal to ask him a question and hear him say, "Great question." So, I asked him: if he was to ask a question to anyone alive or dead, who would it be, why, and what question would he ask them? (I highly encourage you to listen to his answer.) To which he said, "Great questions"—I was overjoyed!

At the very end of our conversation, Tony said, "Jay, keep up the great work. I know you're reaching people all over the world, and I feel your passion and sincerity. Those two things matched together will only serve to help many people. So, blessings to you, brother."

After I stopped recording the podcast, I showed Tony my wish list. He said, "I see you've got Steven Spielberg on your list; you'll get him."

Then we parted ways.

I have so many more stories much like what happened with Joel, Matthew, and Tony, and just how people have believed in what I'm trying to do with *The Story Box* and where it's going.

You can't give up hope; you just can't!

If a twenty-four-year-old can create a top-four podcast in 2021 from his small home office starting out with an iPad Pro, poor audio equipment, and no experience at all and have meaningful conversations or ask the right questions to people, then just think of what you too can achieve!

If I can overcome the rejections, the anxiety of when guests don't show up (and trust me: there have been many of those), and not knowing what to do, then you can also do anything you set your mind to. You've just got to take the first step and strap yourself in tight, because it's going to be one hell of a bumpy but incredibly life-changing ride.

You got this!

COVID-19 was a blessing in disguise for *The Story Box*, and even though the pandemic has impacted people in many ways—some terrible, and my heart does go out to everyone affected in a negative way—*The Story Box* wouldn't have grown the way it has without this global event. In 2020, I did over four hundred interviews with people from every single profession imaginable. I got to listen to and unbox stories from people I never even thought I'd have the opportunity to speak with until *The Story Box* was more well-known.

The only real limit to what you'll be able to achieve lies with your willpower to be persistent and your determination to get back up after being knocked down—to soar like an eagle.

CHAPTER 11

The Path of an Eagle

It's Time for You to Soar

I want to start this final chapter with a question. It's a question I ask my guests on *The Story Box*, and it's one of my all-time favorite questions. It causes people to reflect deeply about their lives, where they are currently, and where they are going—the kind of impacts they want to have on people's lives, whether good or bad. It's my *legacy question*.

Imagine that you have been able to reach the age of one hundred. And as a gift, your family and friends decide to put together a film for you of everything you have ever said and done. And they show it to you on your birthday. It's called your legacy video.

What do you want that film to say and show about your life?

This is a hypothetical question, but it gets you thinking about the kind of life you want to live and leave behind for people to remember you by. In other words: what kind of leader do you want to be remembered as?

A Good Leader of Change

I want people to see that I was a good leader, despite all the struggles, obstacles, pain, suffering, disappointments, and proud moments.

Andrew Scipione said, "Jarred, everyone is a leader. The choice is whether you are going to be a good one or a bad one."

I don't want to lead people away from the truth. I want to show them by my example how they can live life filled with fulfillment, joy, and happiness. The path of an eagle is one carved with righteous leaders, the ones who when knocked down, don't stay down—they continue to get back up again. That's what I want my life to show people.

That has been the theme throughout this whole book.

I have a picture framed on my wall at home about two kinds of leaders. The top image depicts one leader calling all the shots to those in front of him. That leader is known as a boss. The bottom image shows the true example of what a leader is. He's leading from the front—he isn't barking orders; he's showing up with his strength, mind, and will. That is what I want people to see: no matter what Jay went through, he kept on showing up.

God intended for an eagle to soar in the heavens and not be stuck on the ground. I read a powerful fable about an eagle once that challenged my perspective about change and leadership.

I left the best eagle stories for last...

The fable goes like this. Did you know that an eagle can live up to seventy years? However, by the time it reaches the age of forty, the eagle's talons don't grip as well, and the beak becomes bent from overuse and old age. The eagle has only two options at this stage. It can either go and die or go through a painful process of change.

Leaders also have two options when faced with halting circumstances. Give up or adapt and work through the painful change.

The process for the eagle involves it flying up to the top of a mountain. There it sits on its nest. The eagle will then bang its beak against a rock until the beak falls off. The eagle then starts plucking out its old-aged feathers. This process can last 150 days or five months, but eventually, the eagle is reborn once again. It grows a new beak, talons, and feathers. After this process is complete, the eagle can live for another thirty years.

I feel like I've gone through many life-changing painful experiences. Each one has given me the ability to further open my mind to greater possibilities and life lessons. These experiences have taught me that leaders can't avoid change, good or bad, but we can choose to expand our thoughts, remove limiting beliefs, and allow ourselves the renewed strength to soar high like an eagle.

The eagle is a master of managing change. When it's time for an eaglet to learn how to fly, the mother starts removing all the comfortable layers in her nest. She exposes sharp sticks and pricks. The mother then begins throwing her young out of the nest. Out of fear, the eaglets jump back into the nest but are pricked by the sharp sticks and objects. The mother doesn't give up though and continues throwing her young out of the nest until they start flapping their wings.

While this is just a fictional story. The lesson is simple yet powerful.

We mustn't hang on to what is old and familiar to us. We need to step outside of our comfort zones right into the heart of the unfamiliar and fail numerous times in order to learn more than before. Growth is painful but necessary.

Leaders encourage change because they know that, at the end of it, there is real strength. I want people to look back on my life and see that my strength was built over time from all the painful and not so painful changes I experienced. I want people to remember me as a good leader.

A Committed Leader

If you won't commit, you won't persist. It's a fact. An eagle loves to test the level of commitment before it engages in anything. The female eagle will test the level of commitment of her male to see if he is best suited for her. The lesson here is that it's wiser to see whether someone is committed or not before entering into partnership with them. It's about establishing trust because if no one can trust you as a leader, you aren't leading anyone.

I hope that my legacy video captures how whenever I made a commitment to something or someone, I honored it and that people trusted me.

Leaders Love Storms

Eagles love storms! When the storm clouds appear, the eagle gets excited because it knows the storm winds will propel it above the clouds. Once the eagle is soaring high above the clouds, it can rest. With rest comes renewed strength to continue forward. Challenges like I mentioned in this book will bring more opportunities than you can imagine. I know it's never easy, but we can all learn from the eagle.

I want my legacy video to acknowledge that, even though I worked hard, when challenges came, I delighted in them because I was then able to rest, readjust, and refocus.

A Leader of Successful Habits

Did you know that good leaders will create habits in their lives and perform them daily to inspire the right kind of change in not only themselves but those around them? An eagle is a creature of habit too; it wakes up early before all other birds to begin hunting for breakfast.

Back in 2017, when I endured my bowel blockage, I stayed up all night with a restless mind. I sat in my chair overlooking Sydney's beautiful Harbour Bridge and Centrepoint Tower. I watched the sun gradually rise that morning and it was a beautiful transitioning period for me. I realized something special that day. I no longer had a restless mind, and the pain that I was experiencing was gone—I felt on top of the world. In that very moment, I felt at peace. It was a feeling I had not experienced for quite some time.

The sun is a constant thing. Every single day without fail, it will rise and give the world light. I decided in that hospital room that if I could beat the sun and wake up before it, no matter what came my way that day, I could beat it too. I may not have the best of days every day, but I go to bed knowing that tomorrow, the sun will rise anew and so will I.

This has been a habit of mine for three years now, and I have no intention of stopping. I haven't missed a sunrise yet. Even when it is raining outside, I will still get up before the sun and do my morning habits before everyone else's day gets started. You might be wondering what this involves...

I get up every morning at 4 a.m., without fail. However, if I am tired from the day before, I will wake up at 4:30 a.m. I then spend at least thirty minutes praying and reading a verse or chapter from my Bible and meditating on the words.

Come 5 a.m., I'm usually out the door pounding the pavement, either walking or running for forty to fifty minutes. I love listening to podcasts on my walks or runs, as it gives my brain more time to learn and grow while moving. There is science-backed research that when you are moving while listening to or watching something, you'll remember it more.

I will then do a CrossFit-style high-intensity workout outside for at least thirty-five minutes while watching the sun come up. (At least on the days I'm blessed to see the sun.) This helps to strengthen my bones and build up my muscles. When I get home at around 7 a.m., it's time to get ready for work.

I want to be remembered for committing to my habits daily because they helped bring me success, happiness, fulfillment, and joy every day.

Leaders Show Love

What is love? It's an interesting question, isn't it? There are so many different types of love—from unconditional to romantic to *agape*. We all crave that deep, underlying emotional sense and feeling that indicates to us that it must be love. All of us at one stage or another have had a conversation surrounding the definition of what love really is. What do you think it is?

Neuroscientists say that love makes your hormones go crazy, and you become addicted to either another human or object. Science will also tell you that love is a bunch of chemical releases, such as dopamine, oxytocin, and serotonin, in the brain. Therefore, love can be enticingly addictive for many people, and I'm including myself in that statement too.

Here is what I believe love is. I believe that God is love and therefore, we can love deeper than we ever have before because He first loved us.

Imagine that somebody you didn't know sacrificed themselves so that you could live longer. How would that make you feel? I wouldn't even know how to react, to be completely honest. To think that someone would just give up their life for the sake of my own. How do you comprehend that? But that's what a good leader does—they sacrifice time, money, energy, and sometimes their life for the sake of another.

You see, I believe that love is more than just chemicals roaming around in our brains. No, it's far greater and far more special than we realize. For example, if a mother eagle's eaglet is in any kind of danger, she will rush to defend it, and if it comes down to it, she will give up her life in the process.

Leaders *show* love; they don't just *feel* it.

When I reach the end of my life, I want people to know that I loved sacrificially, that I kept on giving even when I couldn't give any more. I want to lead by showing love to people, especially those whose hearts are in pain and discomfort. I know that the love I try my best to give while here on this Earth will help change lives for good.

Leaders Make a Difference

Nothing else really matters to me more than leaving this world knowing that I did all I could to spread the gospel of Jesus Christ. I want to know that I not only shared it—I lived it with every thought, word, and deed. Leaders make a positive difference in the lives of those around them.

So I hope that the final part of my legacy video, titled *The Path of an Eagle: How to Overcome and Lead after Being Knocked Down*, would capture how I made a difference for Christ. How I was able to show others what it takes to overcome life's greatest challenges and lead a life to the full.

I want to end this book and chapter with some of the other most important questions I can ever ask anyone. If Christ was to come back today, do you know him as your Lord and Savior? I spoke about faith in an earlier chapter and how it's very real. Do you believe that God loves you enough that he sent his only son Jesus who willingly gave up his life to die for your sin and the sin of all humankind, past, present, and future?

Do you understand that Jesus didn't stay dead, but he rose again on the third day? He conquered death for you. He went through the worst treatment for you. He did that out of love for you. Jesus is the ultimate leader we should always choose to follow.

My final question to you is this: will you accept him into your life today? The Bible says in Romans 10:13: "For whosoever shall call upon the name of the Lord shall be saved."

It's your choice to accept Jesus into your heart and life. But trust me, I wouldn't be here today if it weren't for Jesus. I owe him everything and he owes me nothing. He has given me the best life ever.

I have decided to take the path of an eagle. I won't turn back, I won't give in, I won't stay on the ground. I will continue to put my hope and trust in God because I know he will renew my strength every single time I get knocked down; he will enable me to get back up and soar on the wings like an eagle. I will run and never get tired again; I will lead and not be faint.

Will you join me by choosing to take the path of an eagle?

Don't wait any longer because it's time for you to soar high in your life.

So, soar high my friends...I'll meet you above the clouds.

Be forever blessed.

Your friend,

Jay

CONNECT WITH JAY!

Facebook: https://www.facebook.com/thestoryboxpodcast

Website: https://thestoryboxpodcast.com/

Instagram: https://www.instagram.com/iamjayfantom/

LinkedIn: https://www.linkedin.com/in/jay-fantom-91a6b96b/

AFTERWORD

By Fiona Fantom

I am reminded of this Bible verse when I think of the journey Jay has been on since birth.

> "Who comforteth us in all our tribulation, that we may be able to comfort them which are in any trouble, by the comfort wherewith we ourselves are comforted of God."
>
> —2 Corinthians 1:4 (KJV)

As you have read, Jay's life has had some twists and turns—some from his own choices and others from God—that have allowed for his greater purpose.

As Jay's mom, I would like to peel away the layers of a young man who I believe has exemplified this Bible verse from a very young age.

Jay has always loved stories and was eager to learn how to read. When I would read to him, he would immerse himself in the story, letting his imagination run wild, asking questions, and always empathizing with the characters.

And even before he could write, there was nothing stopping his creative mind from making up stories and sharing them with anyone who would listen. I believe God gave him this desire to share stories, which in turn lay the foundation to grow and gift him with these talents on his life journey.

⌒◿◿◿◿◯

I would like to take you back to some examples of Jay's heart from when he was young.

It was what we called a "normal day" in the Fantom house. It was the Monday before Easter. I picked up Jay and his brother Nathan from school, and all the way home, Jay was rattled and wouldn't stop talking about the injustice of why some of his kindergarten classmates believed in the Easter bunny and not Jesus.

Jay kept saying, "Mommy, Easter is about Jesus, not chocolate!"

To put this into perspective, Jay had not long received Jesus as his Savior, and he was keen to let everyone know how they could go to heaven. His little heart was genuinely concerned; however, his classmates weren't interested.

We weren't home for long, and Jay came to me in the kitchen with his hands on his hips, pacing (this was the norm when he wanted to make a statement), and said, "Mommy, you have to help me, and I just don't know what to do."

I took him into the living room, and I sat at the computer desk and said, "We will pray, and God will guide Mommy in helping you."

After we prayed, I looked outside to the garden area—not at anything particular—and just asked God to show me a way to help Jay. When I lifted my eyes, I saw a small cocoon hanging on the fence. I then pondered the journey of the butterfly, which resembles the transformation a person goes through when they trust Jesus to be their Savior. Immediately, I knew this was from God and I needed to write a poem to reflect this for Jay.

Within one hour, God had given me the poem and the idea for Jay and me to bake some butterfly cakes and send these to school. Well, Jay was over the moon, but wasn't satisfied with just that. He organized with the principal for me to come and read the poem to the children in his class for Easter and give them an illustration of how a butterfly comes to be. I also ran a playgroup in our church, so I was able to use this for the children as well.

God saw the heart of a child wanting to help his friends know about Jesus, and God answered his prayer.

Jay's desire to help his friends inspired me, and it wasn't long after this that God gave me two more poems with different characters to write about. These will become a series and are currently in the illustration stage. I'm waiting on the Lord to have these published for children. Only God knows the fruit that will come from this.

A few years later, when our youngest son Jonny started school, the Lord provided me a part-time job at the school. Our school wasn't very big, so everyone knew each other. I'm sure Jay spent every recess and lunch looking for students that had hurt themselves or were sick. He would burst through the front office door with the patient, saying, "Mommy, I've got another one for you to fix," and then he would watch me intently while patting the student on the back and telling them they were going to be okay.

Life has certainly been interesting with Jay, and he has this desire and gift to help people in unique ways.

When we learned that our youngest had special needs, the Lord directed Jay to use his creative writing and film experience to create short films and enter them into the NOVA

Employment Focus on Ability competitions to raise awareness for people with disabilities.

Jay's podcast—*The Story Box*—is no different. God is opening the doors. We are very proud of Jay and thankful to God for Jay's persistent, consistent, and resilient "get back up again" mindset.

We're looking forward to seeing where God will take him, believing that whoever comes across Jay's path will be a recipient of this young man's wisdom beyond his years. Our son has a heart that is set on helping others in any way he can.

The Path of an Eagle is only the beginning.

May you learn from Jay's journey because this book was written just for you.

BOOK RECOMMENDATIONS

I love to read. My editor thought it would be a great idea to put together a list of some of my favorite books. It's hard to pick favorites, so these recommendations are in no specific order.

1. *The King James Bible*
2. *Greenlights* by Matthew McConaughey
3. *The Relentless Courage of a Scared Child* by Tana Amen
4. *How To Do the Work* by Dr. Nicole LePera
5. *Excellence Wins* by Horst Schulze
6. *Hope Heals* and *Suffer Strong* by Katherine and Jay Wolf
7. *The Body Keeps the Score* by Bessel van der Kolk
8. *You're Not Broken* by Dr. Sarah Woodhouse
9. *A Woman Makes a Plan* by Maye Musk
10. *The Attributes* by Rich Diviney
11. *Change Your World* by John C. Maxwell and Rob Hoskins (or any of John Maxwell's books)
12. *Man Enough* by Justin Baldoni
13. *Chatter* by Dr. Ethan Kross
14. *The Proof is in the Plants* by Simon Hill
15. *Atomic Habits* by James Clear
16. *Get Out of Your Own Way* by Dave Hollis
17. *On the Edge* by Alison Levine
18. *Selflovology* by Armon Anderson
19. *Woman Evolve* by Sarah Jakes Roberts

20. *The Gift* and *The Choice* by Dr. Edith Eger
21. *Man's Search for Meaning* by Viktor Frankl
22. *The Boy, The Mole, The Fox and The Horse* by Charlie Mackesy
23. *Shoemaker* by Joe Foster
24. *Can't Hurt Me* by David Goggins
25. *Everybody, Always* and *Dream Big* by Bob Goff, and *Love Does* by Bob Goff and Donald Miller
26. *Signs of Hope* by Amy Wolff
27. *Life is Magic* by Jon Dorenbos and Larry Platt
28. *Loving What Is* by Byron Katie
29. *Start With Why* by Simon Sinek
30. *That Will Never Work* by Marc Randolph
31. *Why We Sleep* by Matthew Walker
32. *The Path* by Peter Mallouk and Tony Robbins
33. *Breath* by James Nestor
34. *The Ride of a Lifetime* by Robert Iger
35. *The Happiest Man on Earth* by Eddie Jaku
36. *Ancient Remedies* by Dr. Josh Axe
37. *The Energy Paradox* and *The Plant Paradox* by Dr. Steven Gundry
38. *Think Like a Monk* by Jay Shetty
39. *The Gift of Forgiveness* by Katherine Schwarzenegger Pratt
40. *Tuesdays with Morrie, The Stranger in the Lifeboat, Finding Chika,* and *The Five People You Meet in Heaven* by Mitch Albom
41. *Cleaning Up Your Mental Mess* by Dr. Caroline Leaf
42. *Don't Sweat the Small Stuff* by Richard Carlson
43. *The Mask of Masculinity* by Lewis Howes
44. *The Monk Who Sold His Ferrari* and *The 5 AM Club* by Robin Sharma
45. *Just Mercy* by Bryan Stevenson

46. *Money: Master the Game* by Tony Robbins
47. *How Far You Have Come* by Morgan Harper Nichols
48. *12 Rules for Life* and *Beyond Order*
    by Dr. Jordan B. Peterson
49. *Limitless* by Jim Kwik
50. *The 7 Habits of Highly Successful People* and
    The Speed of Trust by Stephen M. R. Covey
51. *The Energy Bus* by Jon Gordon
52. *Pivot & Go* by David Nurse
53. *Twelve Pillars* by Jim Rohn
54. *Never Split the Difference* by
    Christopher Voss and Tahl Raz
55. *The Alchemist* by Paulo Coelho
56. *The Gifts of Imperfections* by Brené
    Brown (or any Brené Brown books)
57. *Fighting For Life* by Lila Rose
58. *Live Free* by DeVon Franklin
59. *Winning* by Tim Grover and Shari Wenk
60. *Relationship Goals* by Pastor Michael Todd
61. *You Are Never Alone* and *How Happiness
    Happens* or any books by Max Lucado
62. *The Way of Integrity* by Martha Beck
63. *Feel Good Fables* by Nancy J. Ganz
64. *On My Own Two Feet* by Amy Purdy
65. *The Seven Longest Yards* by Chris and Emily Norton
66. *Rock Bottom to Rock Star* by Ryan Blair
67. Christine Caine books—any of them!
68. *Super Attractor* and *The Universe Has
    Your Back* by Gabby Bernstein
69. *The 5-Day Real Food Detox* by Nikki Sharp
70. *Dying to Be Me* by Anita Moorjani
71. *Way of The Peaceful Warrior* by Dan Millman
72. *Rich Dad Poor Dad* by Robert T. Kiyosaki

73. *Happy* by Turia Pitt
74. *Finding Your Harmony* by Ally Brooke
75. *Professional Troublemaker* by Luvvie Ajayi Jones
76. Najwa Zebian books—any of them!
77. Mark Manson books—any of them!
78. *The Gift of Failure* and *The Addiction Inoculation* by Jessica Lahey
79. Johann Hari books—any of them!
80. Jon Acuff books—any of them!
81. Dr. Shefali Tsabary books—any of them!
82. *Set Boundaries, Find Peace* by Nedra Tawwab
83. *Finding Ultra* and *Voicing Change* by Rich Roll
84. *Will* by Will Smith
85. *The Midnight Library* by Matt Haig
86. *In Order to Live* by Yeonmi Park and Maryanne Vollers
87. *The High 5 Habit* by Mel Robbins
88. *God, Do You Hear Me?* by Pastor Derwin Gray
89. *Divine Disruption* by The Evans Family
90. *Married Sex* by Gary Thomas and Debra Fileta
91. *Peak Mind* by Dr. Amishi P. Jha
92. *A Hunter-Gatherer's Guide to the 21st Century* by Bret Weinstein and Heather Heying
93. *Courage is Calling* by Ryan Holiday
94. *Made by Morgan* by Morgan Hipworth
95. *A Surrendered Yes* by Rebekah Lyons
96. *Beyond Happiness* by Jenn Lim
97. *Let Them Lead* by John U. Bacon
98. *No Bullsh!t Leadership* by Martin G. Moore
99. *Live No Lies* by John Mark Comer
100. *Redeeming Your Time* by Jordan Raynor
101. *The Girl With Seven Names* by Hyeonseo Lee with David John